Portuguese
Phrase Book
&
Dictionary

Berlitz Publishing
New York   Munich   Singapore

Contacting the Editors
Every effort has been made to provide accurate information in this publication, but changes are inevitable. The publisher cannot be responsible for any resulting loss, inconvenience or injury. We would appreciate it if readers would call our attention to any errors or outdated information. We also welcome your suggestions; if you come across a relevant expression not in our phrasebook, please contact us: Berlitz Publishing, 193 Morris Avenue, Springfield, NJ 07081, USA. Email: comments@berlitzbooks.com

Third Printing: July 2009
Printed in Singapore

Publishing Director: Sheryl Olinsky Borg
Senior Editor: Lorraine Sova
Editor/Project Manager: Emily Bernath
Translation: GGP Publishing, Anthony Feire
Composition: Datagrafix, Inc.
Cover Design: Claudia Petrilli
Interior Design: Derrick Lim, Juergen Bartz
Production Manager: Elizabeth Gaynor
Cover Photo: © Alamer/Iconotec/age fotostock
Interior Photos: p. 14 © Studio Fourteen/Brand X Pictures/age fotostock; p. 19 © European Central Bank; p. 29 © Pixtal/age fotostock; p. 38 © Roman Krochuk, 2006/Shutterstock, Inc.; p. 41 © Corbis/fotosearch.com; p. 54 © Purestock/Alamy; p. 60 © YinYang/2007 iStock international, Inc.; p. 63 © Stockbyte Photography/2002-07 Veer Incorporated; p. 80 © Graca Victoria, 2007 Used under license from Shutterstock, Inc.; p. 86 © Javier Larrea/Pixtal/age fotostock; p. 89 © Netfalls, 2007 Used under license from Shutterstock, Inc.; p. 108 © rubiphoto, 2007 Used under license from Shutterstock, Inc.; p. 112 © Imageshop.com; p. 117 © image100/Corbis; p. 119 © Renaud Visage/age fotostock; p. 123, 126 © 2007 Jupiterimages Corporation; p. 133 © Clara Natoli, 2007 Used under license from Shutterstock, Inc.; p. 142 © 2007 Jupiterimages Corporation; p. 151 © Jupiterimages/Brand X/Corbis; p. 153 © Stockbyte/Fotosearch.com; p. 156 © Corbis/2006 Jupiterimages Corporation; p. 159 © David McKee/2003-2007 Shutterstock, Inc.; p. 160, 164, 180 © 2007 Jupiterimages Corporation; inside back cover: © H.W.A.C.

Contents

Survival

Food

People

Fun

Special Needs

Resources

Pronunciation

This section is designed to make you familiar with the sounds of Portuguese using our simplified phonetic transcription. You'll find the pronunciation of the Portuguese letters and sounds explained below, together with their "imitated" equivalents. This system is used throughout the phrase book; simply read the pronunciation as if it were English, noting any special rules below.

Stressed syllables are indicated by underlining in the phonetics. Portuguese has four accent marks; acute (´), grave (`), circumflex (ˆ), and tilde (˜). Accent marks are used to indicate a stressed syllable, or to distinguish between words with the same spelling but with a different pronunciation and meaning: for example, **é** pronounced "eh" (meaning is) and **e** pronounced "ee" (meaning and).

There are some differences in vocabulary and pronunciation between the Portuguese spoken in Portugal and that spoken in Brazil, although people in either country can easily understand the other. This book is specifically geared to travelers in Portugal, with Brazilian equivalents shown in brackets.

Consonants

Letter(s)	Approximate Pronunciation	Symbol	Example	Pronunciation
b	1. as in English	b	**bota**	<u>baw</u>·tuh
	2. between vowels, as in English but softer	b	**bebida**	beh·<u>bee</u>·duh
c	1. before e or i, like s in same	s	**centro**	<u>sehn</u>·troh
	2. like k in kit	k	**como**	<u>koh</u>·moh
ç	like s in same	s	**cabeça**	kuh·<u>beh</u>·suh

7

Letter(s)	Approximate Pronunciation	Symbol	Example	Pronunciation
ch	like sh in shower	sh	**chave**	shahv
d	1. as in English	d	**diário**	dee·ah·ree·oo
	2. like th in theater	th	**medo**	meh·thoo
g	1. before e or i, like s in pleasure	zs	**gelo**	zseh·loo
	2. before a, e or u, as in English	g	**guerra**	geh·rruh
h	always silent		**história**	ee·staw·ree·uh
j	like s in pleasure	zs	**juiz**	zsoo·eezs
l	1. as in English	l	**luz**	looz
	2. before h (lh), like ll in millions	ly	**milho**	mee·lyoo
m	1. as in English	m	**camera**	cuh·meh·ruh
	2. at the end of a word, m is nasalized: see p. 11			
n	1. as in English	n	**caneta**	kuh·neh·tah
	2. before h (nh), like ny in canyon	ny	**banho**	buh·nyoo
qu	1. before e and i, like k in kite	k	**quente**	kint
	2. before a and o like qu in queen	kw	**qualidade**	kwah·lee·dahd
r	1. strongly trilled	rr	**rio**	rree·oo
	2. lightly trilled	r	**para**	puh·ruh

Letter(s)	Approximate Pronunciation	Symbol	Example	Pronunciation
s	1. like s in same	s	**sua**	<u>soo</u>·uh
	2. between vowels, like z in zebra	z	**camisa**	kuh·<u>mee</u>·zuh
x	1. like sh in sheep	sh	**peixe**	paysh
	2. like s in same	s	**próximo**	<u>praw</u>·see·moo
	3. like z in lazy	z	**exame**	ee·<u>zuhm</u>

Letters f, m, p, t and z are pronounced as in English. Letters k, w and y are used only in foreign loan words.

Vowels

Letter(s)	Approximate Pronunciation	Symbol	Example	Pronunciation
a, ã, â	like a in about	uh	**anos**	<u>uh</u>·nooz
á, à	like a in father	ah	**farmácia**	fuhr·<u>mah</u>·see·uh
e	1. like e in get	eh	**esta**	<u>eh</u>·stuh
	2. like ee in eel	ee	**exame**	ee·<u>zuhm</u>
	3. silent at the end of a word		**leite**	layt
	4. occasionally, like i in inn	i	**antes**	<u>ahn</u>·tis
	5. when combined with the letter l, like ay in say	ay	**leite**	layt
é	like e in get	eh	**esta**	<u>eh</u>·stuh

Letter(s)	Approximate Pronunciation	Symbol	Example	Pronunciation
ê	like i in inn	i	**mês**	miz
i, í	like ee in eel	ee	**sim**	seeng
o	1. like au in caught	au	**onda**	<u>aun</u>·duh
	2. at the end of a word, like oo in boo	oo	**gato**	<u>gah</u>·too
oi	like oy in coy	oy	**doi**	doy
ó	like aw in paw	aw	**história**	ee·<u>staw</u>·ree·uh
ô	like u in put	oah	**avô**	uh·<u>voah</u>
u	1. like oo in boo	oo	**uva**	<u>oo</u>·vuh
	2. silent after g and q		**guerra**	<u>geh</u>·rruh
ú	like oo in boo	oo	**úmido**	<u>oo</u>·mee·thoo

When a vowel has an accent, you must stress the syllable in the word that contains the accented vowel.

Nasal Sounds

Some nasal sounds are produced when a vowel is followed by the letter m. This nasal sound is also found when a combination of certain vowels are used (ãe, ão, õe). These nasal sounds produce either an ng sound (e.g., tying) or an oam sound (e.g., foam) with the speaker barely pronouncing the g or m.

Letter(s)	Approximate Pronunciation	Symbol	Example	Pronunciation
ãe	like ayin in saying	eng	**mãe**	meng
ão	like oam in foam	ohm	**cão**	kohm
õe	like oing in boing	oing	**milhões**	mee·<u>lyoings</u>

Letter(s)	Approximate Pronunciation	Symbol	Example	Pronunciation
am	at the end of a word, like oam in foam otherwise not nasal: see page 8	ohm	**falam**	<u>fah</u>·loam
om	like ong in gong	ohng	**som**	sohng
em	like aying in saying	eng	**bem**	beng
im	like ing in tying	ing	**assim**	uh·<u>sing</u>

i

There are over 230 million speakers of Portuguese worldwide. Portuguese is the sixth most spoken language in the world, and there are 188 million speakers of Portuguese in South America alone. It is the official language of Angola, Brazil, Cape Verde, East Timor, Guinea-Bissau, Mozambique, Portugal and São Tomé and Príncipe. Listed below is an approximation of the numbers of Portuguese speakers in the various countries:

Portuguese is also spoken in Macao, though Cantonese is the language of commerce. There are about 400,000 Portuguese speakers in the United States.

How to Use This Book

These essential phrases can also be heard on the audio CD.

Sometimes you see two alternatives in italics, separated by a slash. Choose the one that's right for your situation.

Essential

Where is the *market/mall [shopping center]*?	**Onde é *o mercado/a zona comercial*?** aund eh *oo mehr·kah·thoo/uh zau·nuh koo·mehr·see·ahl*
I'm just looking.	**Estou só a ver [vendo].** ee·<u>stawoo</u> saw uh vehr [<u>vehn</u>·doo]

Portuguese words shown in brackets are Brazilian.

Pode ajudar-me? pawd uh·zsoo·<u>dahr</u>·meh

You May See...

EMPURRAR/PUXAR	push/pull
CASA DE BANHO [O BANHEIRO]/LAVAROS	bathroom/restroom [toilet]

Ticketing

When's...	**A que horas é...** uh kee <u>aw</u>·ruhz eh...
– the (first) bus	– **a (primeira) camioneta [o (primeiro) ônibus]** uh (pree·<u>may</u>·ruh) kah·meeoo·<u>neh</u>·tuh [oo (pree·<u>may</u>·roo) <u>aw</u>·nee·boos]
– the (next) flight	– **o (próximo) vôo** oo (<u>praw</u>·see·moo) <u>vau</u>·oo
– the (last) train	– **o (último) comboio [trem]** oo (<u>ool</u>·tee·moo) kaum·<u>baw</u>·eeoo

Words you may see are shown in *You May See* boxes.

Any of the words or phrases preceded by dashes can be plugged into the sentence above.

12

Portuguese phrases appear in red.

Read the simplified pronunciation as if it were English. For more on pronunciation, see page 7.

Relationships

Who are you with?	**Com quem está?** kaun keng ee·<u>stah</u>
I'm on my own.	**Estou sozinho** ♂/**sozinha** ♀. ee·<u>stawoo</u> saw·<u>zee</u>·nyoo ♂/saw·<u>zee</u>·nyuh ♀
I'm with my...	**Estou com.**

When different gender forms apply, the masculine form is followed by ♂; feminine by ♀.

– husband/wife	– **marido/m**...ehr
– boyfriend/girlfriend	– **namorad**...noo/ nuh·moo·<u>rah</u>...
– friend(s)	– **amigo(s)** ♂/**amiga(s)** ♀ uh·<u>mee</u>·goo(z) ♂/uh·<u>mee</u>·guh(z) ♀

▶ For numbers, see page 177.

The arrow indicates a cross reference where you'll find related phrases.

Information boxes contain relevant country, culture and language tips.

i Street Markets are an integral part of Portuguese life, but you must get there early to get the full experience. By 10:00 a.m. the best things are gone.

You May Hear...

O que deseja? oo keh deh·<u>zeh</u>·zsuh	What would you like?
Recomendo... reh·koo·<u>mehn</u>·doo...	I recommend...
Bom apetite. bohng uh·peh·<u>tee</u>·teh	Enjoy your meal.

Expressions you may hear are shown in *You May Hear* boxes.

Color-coded side bars identify each section of the book.

13

▼ Survival

Essential

I'm on *vacation [holiday]/business*.

Estou *de férias/em negócios*. ee-<u>stawoo</u> deh <u>feh</u>-ree-uhz/eng neh-<u>gaw</u>-see-yooz

I'm going to…

Vou para… vawoo <u>puh</u>-ruh…

I'm staying at the… Hotel.

Permaneço no hotel… pehr-muh-<u>neh</u>-soo noo aw-<u>tehl</u>…

You May Hear…

O seu *bilhete/passaporte*. oo sehoo <u>bee</u>-<u>lyeht</u>/ <u>pah</u>-suh-pawrt

Your *ticket/passport*, please.

O que é o propósito de sua visita? oo kee eh oo prau-<u>paw</u>-zee-too deh <u>soo</u>-uh vee-<u>zee</u>-tuh

What's the purpose of your visit?

Onde está a ficar [ficando]? aund ee-<u>stah</u> uh fee-<u>kahr</u> [fee-<u>kuhn</u>-doo]

Where are you staying?

Quanto tempo vai ficar? <u>kwuhn</u>-too <u>tehm</u>-poo veye fee-<u>kahr</u>

How long are you staying?

Com quem está? kohm keng ee-<u>stah</u>

Who are you with?

Passport Control and Customs

I'm just passing through.

Estou só de passagem. ee-<u>stawoo</u> saw deh puh-<u>sah</u>-zheng

I would like to declare…

Queria declarar… keh-<u>ree</u>-uh deh-kluh-<u>rahr</u>…

I have nothing to declare.

Não tenho nada a declarar. nohm <u>teh</u>-nyoo <u>nah</u>-duh uh deh-kluh-<u>rahr</u>

You May Hear...

Tem alguma coisa a declarar? teng
ahl·<u>goo</u>·muh <u>koy</u>·zuh uh deh·kluh·<u>rahr</u>

Do you have
anything to declare?

Tem de pagar direitos [alfandegários] nisto.
teng deh puh·<u>gahr</u> dee·<u>ray</u>·tooz
[uhl·fuhn·deh·<u>gah</u>·ree·ooz] <u>nee</u>·stoo

You must pay duty
on this.

Abra este saco, por favor. <u>ah</u>·bruh <u>eh</u>·steh
<u>sah</u>·koo poor fuh·<u>vaur</u>

Please open this
bag.

You May See...

ALFÂNDEGA	customs
MERCADORIA TAXE LIVRE	duty-free goods
ARTIGOS A DECLARAR	goods to declare
NADA A DECLARAR	nothing to declare
CONTROLE DE PASSAPORTES	passport control
POLÍCIA	police

Money and Banking

Essential

Where's...?	**Onde é...?** aund eh...
– the ATM	– **o multibanco [a caixa automática]** oo mool·tee·<u>buhn</u>·koo [uh <u>keye</u>·shuh aw·too·<u>mah</u>·tee·kuh]
– the bank	– **o banco** oo <u>buhn</u>·koo
– the currency exchange office	– **o câmbio** oo <u>kuhm</u>·bee·oo

What time does the bank *open/close*?	**A que horas é que o banco *abre/fecha*?** uh keh <u>aw</u>·ruhz eh keh oo <u>buhn</u>·koo *<u>ah</u>·breh/ <u>feh</u>·shuh*
I'd like to change *dollars/pounds* into *euros/reais*.	**Queria trocar *dólares/libras* em *euros/ reais*.** keh·<u>ree</u>·uh troo·<u>kahr</u> *<u>daw</u>·luhrz/<u>lee</u>·bruhz* eng *<u>ehoo</u>·rooz/rree·<u>eyez</u>*
I want to cash some traveler's checks [cheques].	**Quero cobrar [trocar] cheques de viagem.** <u>keh</u>·roo koo·<u>brahr</u> [troo·<u>kahr</u>] <u>sheh</u>·kehz deh vee·<u>ah</u>·zseng

ATM, Bank and Currency Exchange

Can I exchange foreign currency here?	**Posso trocar divisas [moedas] estrangeiras aqui?** <u>paw</u>·soo troo·<u>kahr</u> dee·<u>vee</u>·zuhz [moo·<u>eh</u>·duhz] ee·struhn·<u>zsay</u>·ruhz uh·<u>kee</u>
What's the exchange rate?	**A como [quanto] está o câmbio?** uh <u>koo</u>·moo [<u>kwuhn</u>·too] ee·<u>stah</u> oo <u>kuhm</u>·bee·oo
How much commission do you charge?	**Quanto cobram de comissão?** <u>kwuhn</u>·too <u>kaw</u>·brohm deh koo·mee·<u>sohm</u>
I've lost my traveler's checks [cheques].	**Perdi o meu livro de cheques.** pehr·<u>dee</u> oo mehoo <u>lee</u>·vroo deh <u>sheh</u>·kehz
My card was lost.	**O meu cartão foi perdido.** oo mehoo kuhr·<u>tohm</u> foy pehr·<u>dee</u>·thoo
My credit card has been stolen.	**Roubaram-me o meu cartão de crédito.** raw·<u>bah</u>·rohm meh oo mehoo kuhr·<u>tohm</u> deh <u>kreh</u>·dee·too
My credit card doesn't work.	**O meu cartão de crédito não funciona.** oo mehoo kuhr·<u>tohm</u> deh <u>kreh</u>·dee·too nohm foon·see·<u>au</u>·nuh

▶For numbers, see page 177.

You May See...

INSERIR O CARTÃO	insert card here
CANCELAR	cancel
APAGUE	clear
ENTRE	enter
PINO	PIN
RETIRE FUNDOS	withdraw funds
DA CONTA CORRENTE	from checking [current account]
DA CONTA DE POUPANÇA	from savings
RECIBO	receipt

i Currency exchange offices (**Câmbio**) can be found in most Portuguese and Brazilian tourist centers; they generally stay open longer than banks, especially during the summer season.

Travel agencies and hotels are other places where you can exchange money, but the rate will not be as good. In heavy tourist areas, you can also find currency exchange machines on the streets. Of course, you should use caution when exchanging money on the street, especially in cities where crime rates are high.

Remember to take your passport with you when you want to change money.

You May See...

In 2002 the currency in most EU countries, including Portugal, changed to the **euro (€)**, divided into 100 **cêntimos** (cents). The currency in Brazil is the **real (R$)**, plural **reais**, divided into 100 **centavos**.

Portugal   Coins: 1, 2, 5, 10, 20, 50 **cêntimos**; €1,2
                    Notes: €5, 10, 20, 50, 100, 200, 500

Brazil   Coins: 1, 5, 10, 25, 50 **centavos**; 1 **R$**
                    Notes: 1, 2, 5, 10, 20, 50, 100 **R$**

Transportation

Essential

How do I get to the city center?	**Como é que vou para o centro da cidade?** <u>kau</u>·moo eh keh vawoo <u>puh</u>·ruh oo <u>sehn</u>·troo duh see·<u>dahd</u>
Where's…?	**Onde está…?** aund ee·<u>stah</u>…
– the airport	– **o aeroporto** oo uh·eh·rau·<u>paur</u>·too
– the train station [the railway station]	– **a estação de caminho de ferro [a estação ferroviária]** uh ee·stuh·<u>sohm</u> deh kuh·<u>mee</u>·nyoo deh <u>feh</u>·rroo [uh ee·stuh·<u>sohm</u> feh·rroo·vee·<u>ah</u>·ree·uh]
– the bus station	– **a estação de camionetas [ônibus]** uh ee·stuh·<u>sohm</u> deh kah·meeoo·<u>neh</u>·tuhz [<u>aw</u>·nee·boos]
– the subway [underground] station	– **a estação de metro** uh ee·stuh·<u>sohm</u> deh <u>meh</u>·troo
How far is it?	**A que distância fica?** uh keh dee·<u>stuhn</u>·see·uh <u>fee</u>·kuh
Where can I buy tickets?	**Onde posso comprar bilhetes?** aund <u>paw</u>·soo kaum·<u>prahr</u> bee·<u>lyehtz</u>
A *one-way [single]/ round-trip [return]* ticket to…	**Um bilhete *de ida/de ida e volta* para…** oong bee·<u>lyeht</u> deh <u>ee</u>·thuh/deh <u>ee</u>·thuh ee <u>vaul</u>·tuh puh·ruh…
How much?	**Quanto custa?** <u>kwuhn</u>·too <u>koo</u>·stuh
Are there any discounts?	**Há descontos?** ah dehs·<u>caun</u>·tooz
Which…?	**Qual…?** kwahl…
– gate	– **porta** <u>port</u>·uh

– line	**– linha** <u>lee</u>·nyuh
– platform	**– plataforma** plah·tuh·<u>fawr</u>·muh
Where can I get a taxi?	**Onde posso apanhar [pegar] um táxi?** aund <u>paw</u>·soo uh·puh·<u>nyar</u> [peh·<u>gahr</u>] oong <u>tahk</u>·see
Please take me to this address.	**Leve-me a esta morada [neste endereço].** <u>leh</u>·veh·meh uh <u>eh</u>·stuh maw·<u>rah</u>·duh [nehst ehn·deh·<u>reh</u>·soo]
Where can I rent a car?	**Onde posso alugar um carro?** aund <u>paw</u>·soo uh·loo·<u>gahr</u> oong <u>kah</u>·rroo
Could I have a map?	**Pode dar-me um mapa.** pawd <u>dahr</u>·meh oong <u>mah</u>·puh

Ticketing

When's…to…?	**A que horas é…para…?** uh kee <u>aw</u>·ruhz eh…<u>puh</u>·ruh…
– the (first) bus	**– a (primeira) camioneta [o (primeiro) ônibus]** uh (pree·<u>may</u>·ruh) kah·meeoo·<u>neh</u>·tuh [oo (pree·<u>may</u>·roo) <u>aw</u>·nee·boos]
– the (next) flight	**– o (próximo) vôo** oo (<u>praw</u>·see·moo) <u>vau</u>·oo
– the (last) train	**– o (último) comboio [trem]** oo (<u>ool</u>·tee·moo) kaum·<u>baw</u>·eeoo [treng]
Where can I buy tickets?	**Onde posso comprar bilhetes?** aund <u>paw</u>·soo kaum·<u>prahr</u> bee·<u>lyehtz</u>
One/Two ticket(s), please.	***Um bilhete/Dois bilhetes, se faz favor.*** *oong bee·<u>lyeht</u>/doyz bee·<u>lyehtz</u> seh fahz fuh·<u>vaur</u>*
For *today/tomorrow.*	**Para *hoje/amanhã.*** <u>puh</u>·ruh *auzseh/uh·muh·<u>nyuh</u>*

▶ For days, see page 181.

▶ For time, see page 179.

A(n)…ticket	**Um bilhete…** oong bee·<u>lyeht</u>…
– one-way [single]	**– de ida** deh <u>ee</u>·thuh
– round-trip [return]	**– de ida e volta** deh <u>ee</u>·thuh ee <u>vaul</u>·tuh
– first-class	**– em primeira classe** eng pree·<u>may</u>·ruh <u>klah</u>·seh
– economy class	**– em classe económica** eng <u>klah</u>·seh eh·koo·<u>naw</u>·mee·kuh
How much?	**Quanto custa?** <u>kwuhn</u>·too <u>koo</u>·stuh
Is there a discount for…?	**Há desconto para…?** ah dehs·<u>kaum</u>·too <u>puh</u>·ruh…
– children	**– crianças** kree·<u>uhn</u>·suhz
– students	**– estudantes** ee·stoo·<u>duhnts</u>
– senior citizens	**– os reformados [idosos]** ooz reh·faur·<u>mah</u>·dooz [ee·<u>daw</u>·zooz]
I have an e-ticket.	**Eu tenho um e-bilhete.** ehoo <u>teh</u>·nyoo oong ee bee·<u>lyeht</u>
Can I buy a ticket on the *bus/train*?	**Posso comprar o bilhete *na camioneta [no ônibus]/no comboio [no trem]*?** <u>paw</u>·soo kaum·<u>prahr</u> oo bee·<u>lyeht</u> *nuh <u>kah</u>·mee·oo·<u>neh</u>·tuh [noo <u>aw</u>·nee·boos]/noo kaum·<u>baw</u>·ee·oo [noo treng]*
I'd like to…my reservation.	**Queria…a minha reserva.** keh·<u>ree</u>·uh…uh <u>mee</u>·nyuh reh·<u>zehr</u>·vuh
– cancel	**– cancelar** kuhn·seh·<u>lahr</u>
– change	**– mudar** moo·<u>dahr</u>
– confirm	**– confirmar** kaum·feer·<u>mahr</u>

Plane

Getting to the Airport

How much is a taxi to the airport?	**Quanto custa um táxi ao aeroporto?** kwuhn·too koo·stuh oong tahk·see ahoo uh·eh·rau·paur·too
To…Airport, please.	**Ao aeroporto de…, por favor** ahoo uh·eh·rau·paur·too deh…poor fuh·vaur
My airline is…	**A minha linha aérea é…** uh mee·nyuh lee·nyuh ah·ehr·ee·uh eh…
My flight leaves at…	**O meu vôo parte ás…** oo meeoo vau·oo pahr·teh ahz…

▶ For time, see page 179.

I'm in a hurry.	**Estou com pressa.** ee·stawoo kaum preh·suh
Can you take an alternate route?	**Pode tomar uma rota alternada?** pawd too·mahr oo·muh raw·tuh ahl·tehr·nah·thuh
Can you drive *faster/ slower*?	**Voçe pode guiar mais *rapido/ devagar*?** vaw·seh pawd gee·ahr meyez *rah·pee·thoo/deh·vuh·gahr*

You May Hear…

Que linha aérea voam? keh lee·nyuh ah·eh·ree·uh vau·ohm	What airline are you flying?
Domestico ou internacional? thoo·meh·stee·koo awoo een·tehr·nuh·seeoo·nahl	Domestic or international?
Que terminal? keh tehr·mee·nahl	What terminal?

You May See...

CHEGADAS	arrivals
EMBARQUE	departures
ENTREGA DE BAGAGEM	baggage claim
VÔOS DOMÉSTICOS	domestic flights
VÔOS INTERNACIONAIS	international flights
REGISTO	check-in desk
REGISTO E-BILHETES	e-ticket check-in
PORTÕES DE PARTIDA	departure gates

Check-in and Boarding

Where is the check-in counter? **Onde é o registro [check in]?** aund eh oo reh·zsee·stroo [check in]

My name is... **Chamo-me... [Meu nome é...]** shuh·moo meh...[mehoo nau·mee eh...]

I'm going to... **Vou para...** vauoo puh·ruh...

How much luggage is allowed? **Quantas bagagems são permitidas?** kwuhn·tuhz buh·gah·zsengs sohm pehr·mee·tee·thuhs

Which *terminal/gate* does flight...leave from? **Qual é *o terminal/a porta do vôo* para...?** kwahl eh *oo tehr·mee·nahl/uh pawr·tuhz thoo vau·oo* puh·ruh...

I'd like *a window/ an aisle* seat. **Queria um lugar *à janela [no corredor]/ na coxia [de corredor]*** keh·ree·uh oong loo·gahr *ah zsuh·neh·luh [noo koo·rreh·daur]/nuh kau·sheeuh [deh koo·rreh·daur]*

When do we *leave/ arrive*? **Quando vamos *partir/chegar*?** kwuhn·doo vuh·mooz *puhr·teer/shee·gahr*

24

| Is flight…delayed? | **Há atraso no vôo…?** ah uh·<u>trah</u>·zoo noo <u>vau</u>·oo… |
| How late will it be? | **Qual é o atraso?** kwahl eh oo uh·<u>trah</u>·zoo |

You May Hear…

Próximo! <u>praw</u>·see·moo	Next!
O seu *bilhete/passaporte*, faz favor. oo sehoo *bee·<u>lyet</u>/pah·suh·<u>pawrt</u>* fahz fuh·<u>vaur</u>	Your *ticket/passport*, please.
Tem baggagem para despachar? teng buh·<u>gah</u>·zseng puh·ruh dehs·puh·<u>shahr</u>	Are you checking any luggage?
Tem excesso de peso na sua bagagem. teng eh·<u>zeh</u>·soo deh <u>peh</u>·zoo nuh <u>soo</u>·uh buh·<u>gah</u>·zseng	You have excess baggage.
Isso é demasiado volumoso para bagagem de mão. ee·soo eh deh·muh·zee·<u>ah</u>·thoo vaw·loo·<u>mau</u>·zoo puh·ruh buh·<u>gah</u>·zseng deh mohm	That's too large for a carry-on [to carry on board].
Foi o senhor ♂/a senhora ♀ quem fez as malas? foy oo see·nyaur ♂/uh see·<u>nyau</u>·ruh ♀ keng fehz uhs <u>mah</u>·luhs	Did you pack these bags yourself?
Alguem deu-lhe alguma coisa para transportar? ahl·<u>geng</u> <u>dehoo</u>·lyeh ahl·<u>goo</u>·muh <u>coy</u>·zuh puh·ruh truhns·pawr·<u>tahr</u>	Did anyone give you anything to carry?
Tire tudo dos bolsos. <u>tee</u>·reh <u>too</u>·thoo dooz <u>bawl</u>·sooz	Empty your pockets.
Tire seus sapatos. <u>tee</u>·reh sehooz suh·<u>pah</u>·tooz	Take off your shoes.
Estamos a embarquar vôo… ee·<u>stuh</u>·mooz uh eng·buhr·<u>kahr</u> <u>vau</u>·oo…	Now boarding flight…

Luggage

Where *is/are*...?	**Onde *é/são*...?** aund *eh/sohm*...
– the luggage carts [trolleys]	– **os carrinhos** ooz kuh·<u>rree</u>·nyos
– the luggage lockers	– **os cacifos de bagagem** ooz kuh·<u>see</u>·fooz deh buh·<u>gah</u>·zseng
– the baggage claim	– **o depósito de bagagem** oo deh·<u>paw</u>·zee·too deh buh·<u>gah</u>·zseng
My luggage has been lost.	**Perdi a minha bagagem.** pehr·<u>dee</u> uh <u>mee</u>·nyuh buh·<u>gah</u>·zseng
My luggage has been stolen.	**Roubaram a minha bagagem.** raw·<u>bah</u>·rohm uh <u>mee</u>·nyuh buh·<u>gah</u>·zseng
My suitcase was damaged.	**A minha mala foi danificada.** uh <u>mee</u>·nyuh <u>mah</u>·luh foy deh·nee·fee·<u>kah</u>·thuh

Finding your Way

Where *is/are*...?	**Onde *é/são*...?** aund *eh/sohm*
– the currency exchange office	– **o câmbio** oo <u>kuhm</u>·bee·oo
– the car rental [hire]	– **o aluguer de carros** oo uh·loo·<u>gehr</u> deh <u>kah</u>·rrooz
– the exit	– **a saída** uh suh·<u>ee</u>·thuh
– the taxis	– **os taxis** ooz <u>tahk</u>·seez
Is there...into town?	**Há...para o centro?** ah...<u>puh</u>·ruh oo <u>sehn</u>·troo
– a bus	– **um autocarro [ônibus]** oong ahoo·too·<u>kah</u>·rroo [<u>aw</u>·nee·boos]
– a train	– **um comboio [trem]** oong kaum·<u>boy</u>·oo [treng]
– a subway [underground]	– **um metro** oong <u>meh</u>·troo

▶ For directions, see page 36.

Train

Where's the nearest train [railway] station?	**Onde está a estação de comboios mais próxima?** aund ee-<u>stah</u> uh ee-stuh-<u>sohm</u> deh kaum-<u>boy</u>-ooz meyez <u>praw</u>-see-muh
How far is it?	**A que distância fica?** uh keh dee-<u>stuhn</u>-see-uh <u>fee</u>-kuh
Where *is/are*...?	**Onde *está/são*...?** aund ee-<u>stah</u>/sohm...
– the ticket office	– **a bilheteira [bilheteria]** uh bee-lyeht-ay-<u>ree</u>-uh [bee-lyeht-eh-<u>ree</u>-uh]
– the information desk	– **as informações** uhz een-foor-muh-<u>soingz</u>
– the luggage lockers	– **os cacifos de bagagem** ooz kuh-<u>see</u>-fooz deh buh-<u>gah</u>-zseng
– the platforms	– **as linhas [plataformas]** uhz <u>lee</u>-nyuhz [plah-tuh-<u>fawr</u>-muhz]

▶ For directions, see page 36.

▶ For ticketing, see page 21.

You May See...

PARA AS LINHAS	to the platforms
INFORMAÇÕES	information
RESERVAS	reservations
CHEGADAS	arrivals
PARTIDAS	departures

Questions

Could I have a schedule [timetable], please?	**Queria um horário, se faz favor.** keh·*ree*·uh oong aw·*rah*·ree·oo seh fahz fuh·*vaur*
How long is the trip [journey]?	**Quanto tempo demora a viagem?** *kwuhn*·too *tehm*·poo deh·*maw*·ruh uh vee·*ah*·zseng
Do I have to change trains?	**Tenho de mudar de comboio [trem]?** *teh*·nyoo deh moo·*dahr* deh kaum·*boy*·oo [treng]

i The Portuguese railway, **Caminhos de Ferro Portugueses (C.P.)**, handles almost all train services in Portugal and totals 1,771 miles of track. Tickets can be purchased and reservations made in travel agencies and at train stations. You may also purchase your ticket on the train and at various **multibancos** (ATMs). Check out the various special prices and travel cards available (for 7, 14 and 21 days). Rates are cheaper on "Blue Days" (**dias azuis**), and a "Gold Card" is available for people over 65.

Lisbon has four main train stations: **Santa Apolónia** (international, northern Portugal), **Cais do Sodré** (Estoril, Cascais, western suburbs), **Rossio** (Sintra and west) and **Sul e Sueste** (Algarve).

In Brazil, the rail network is quite small. The Brazilian railway, **Estrada de Ferro Central do Brasil (E.F.C.B.),** offers few passenger services. The São Paulo–Rio de Janeiro night journey is comfortable but long and expensive.

Departures

Which track [platform] for the train to…?	**De que linha [plataforma] parte o comboio [trem] para…?** deh keh *lee*·nyuh [plah·tuh·*fawr*·muh] pahrt oo kaum·*boy*·oo [treng] *puh*·ruh…

Is this the track [platform] to…?	**É daqui que parte o comboio [trem] para…?** eh duh·<u>kee</u> keh pahrt oo kaum·<u>boy</u>·oo [treng] <u>puh</u>·ruh…
Where is track [platform]…?	**Onde é a linha [plataforma]…?** aund eh uh <u>lee</u>·nyuh [plah·tuh·<u>fawr</u>·muh]…
Where do I change for…?	**Onde é que mudo para…?** aund eh keh <u>moo</u>·thoo <u>puh</u>·ruh…

Boarding

| Is this seat taken? | **Este lugar está ocupado?** ehst loo·<u>gahr</u> ee·<u>stah</u> aw·koo·<u>pah</u>·thoo |
| That's my seat. | **Esse é o meu lugar.** <u>eh</u>·seh eh oo mehoo loo·<u>gahr</u> |

You May Hear…

Todo a bordo! <u>too</u>·thoo uh <u>baur</u>·thoo	All aboard!
Bilhetes, por favor. bee·<u>lyehtz</u> poor fuh·<u>vaur</u>	Tickets, please.
Tem de mudar em… teng deh moo·<u>dahr</u> eng…	You have to change at…
A próxima paragem [parada]… uh <u>praw</u>·see·muh puh·<u>rah</u>·zseng [puh·<u>rah</u>·duh]…	Next stop…

Bus

Where's the bus station?	**Onde é a estação de camionetas [ônibus]?** aund eh uh ee-stuh-<u>sohm</u> deh <u>kah</u>-meeoo-<u>neh</u>-tuhz [<u>aw</u>-nee-boos]
How far is it?	**A que distância fica?** uh keh dee-<u>stuhn</u>-see-uh <u>fee</u>-kuh
How do I get to…?	**Como se vai para…?** <u>kau</u>-moo seh veye <u>puh</u>-ruh…
Does the bus [coach] stop at…?	**A camioneta [O ônibus] pára em…?** uh kah-myoo-<u>neh</u>-tuh [oo <u>aw</u>-nee-boos] <u>pah</u>-ruh eng…
Could you tell me when to get off?	**Pode-me dizer quando eu devo sair?** <u>paw</u>-deh meh dee-<u>zehr</u> <u>kwuhn</u>-doo <u>deh</u>-voo suh-<u>eer</u>
Do I have to change buses?	**Tenho de mudar de autocarro [ônibus]?** teh-nyoo deh moo-<u>dahr</u> deh ahoo-too-<u>kah</u>-rroo [<u>aw</u>-nee-boos]
Stop here, please!	**Pare aqui, por favor!** <u>pah</u>-reh uh-<u>kee</u> poor fuh-<u>vaur</u>

▶ For ticketing, see page 21.

---

i

In Portugal, intercity bus services are frequent and cover most of the country. Some buses are run by the Portuguese Transport Company, **Rodoviária Nacional (R.N.)**, while others are privately owned.

In Brazil, intercity buses are fairly cheap and comfortable, usually with air conditioning. If you are traveling overnight, look for **leitos**, buses with reclining seats, clean sheets and pillows. Tickets are available from bus stations (**rodoviárias**).

You May See...

PARAGEM DE AUTOCARROS [PARADA DE ÔNIBUS]	bus stop
ENTRADA/SAÍDA	enter/exit
MARQUE O SEU BILHETE	stamp your ticket

Subway [Underground]

Where's the nearest subway [underground] station?	**Onde é a estação de metro mais próxima?** aund eh uh ee-stuh-<u>sohm</u> deh <u>meh</u>-troo meyez <u>praw</u>-see-muh
Could I have a map of the subway [underground], please?	**Pode dar-me um mapa do metro, por favor.** pawd <u>dahr</u>-meh oong <u>mah</u>-puh thoo <u>meh</u>-troo poor fuh-<u>vaur</u>
Which line for...?	**Qual é a linha para...?** kwahl eh uh <u>lee</u>-nyuh <u>puh</u>-ruh...
Do I have to transfer [change]?	**Tenho que transferir?** <u>teh</u>-nyoo keh truhns-feh-<u>reer</u>
Is this the subway [train] to...?	**Este comboio [trem] vai para...?** ehst kaum-<u>boy</u>-oo [treng] veye <u>puh</u>-ruh...
Where are we?	**Onde estamos?** aund ee-<u>stuh</u>-mooz

▶For ticketing, see page 21.

---

i The subway system in Lisbon has four main lines and forty-four stations throughout metropolitan Lisbon. Buy a **senha**, single flat-rate ticket, or a booklet of ten tickets at ticket offices or machines, found in every station.

In Brazil, São Paulo, Rio de Janeiro, Belo Horizonte, Porto Alegre and Recife have modern subway systems, though not covering the whole city. Tickets available are: **unitário** (one-way), **múltiplo 2** (round-trip), **múltiplo 10** (ten trips) and **integração** (one metro + one bus).

Boat and Ferry

When is the ferry to…?	**Quando é o barco [a balsa] para…?** kwuhn·doo eh oo <u>bahr</u>·koo [uh <u>bahl</u>·suh] <u>puh</u>·ruh…
Can I take my car?	**Posso louvar o meu carro?** paw·soo loo·<u>vahr</u> oo mehoo <u>kah</u>·rroo

▶ For ticketing, see page 21.

You May See…

BARCO SALVA-VIDAS	life boat
CINTO DE SALVAÇÃO [DE SEGURANÇA]	life jacket

i Popular cruises in Portugal run down the Douro and Tagus rivers and all along the Algarve Coast. The Douro River cruise begins and ends in the city of Porto. A cruise of the Tagus River begins and ends in Lisbon. The Tagus cruise will take you through centuries of history emerging from monuments scattered throughout the hills.

In Brazil there are specially organized cruises in all coastal towns for visits to main beaches and nearby islands. Transport between Belém, Manaus and Santarém can also be done by boat across the Amazon River, departing from **hidroviárias** (ferry terminals); for the long night journey, a hammock on deck is preferable to a hot cabin.

Cruises on the Amazon are run by the state-owned **Empresa de Navegação da Amazônia (E.N.A.S.A.)** and a number of private companies.

Bicycle and Motorcycle

Where can I rent...?	**Onde posso alugar...?** aund <u>paw</u>·soo uh·loo·<u>gahr</u>...
– a *3-/10-speed* bicycle	**– uma bicicleta de** *trêz/dez* **velocidades [marchas]** <u>oo</u>·muh bee·see·<u>kleh</u>·tuh deh *trehz/dehz* veh·<u>law</u>·see·<u>dah</u>·dehz [<u>mahr</u>·shuhz]
– a moped	**– uma lambreta** <u>oo</u>·muh luhm·<u>breh</u>·tuh
– a motorcycle	**– uma motocicleta** <u>oo</u>·muh maw·taw·see·<u>kleh</u>·tuh
How much per *day/week*?	**Quanto custa por** *dia/semana*? kwuhn·too <u>koo</u>·stuh poor *<u>dee</u>·uh/seh·<u>muh</u>·nuh*
Can I have a *helmet/lock*?	**Posso ter um** *capacete/corrente*? <u>paw</u>·soo tehr oong *kuh·puh·<u>seh</u>·the/koo·<u>rrehnt</u>*

Taxi

Where can I get a taxi?	**Onde posso apanhar [pegar] um táxi?** aund <u>paw</u>·soo uh·puh·<u>nyahr</u> [peh·<u>gahr</u>] oong <u>tahk</u>·see
I'd like a taxi *now/for tomorrow at...*	**Queria um táxi** *agora/amanhã ás*... keh·<u>ree</u>·uh oong <u>tahk</u>·see *uh·<u>gaw</u>·ruh/uh·muh·<u>nyuh</u> ahz...*
Pick me up at...*(place/time)*	**Apanha-me** *no/ás*... uh·<u>puh</u>·nyuh·meh *noo/ahz...*
I'm going to...	**Vou para...** <u>vau</u>·oo <u>puh</u>·ruh...
– this address	**– esta morada [neste endereço]** <u>eh</u>·stuh maw·<u>rah</u>·duh [nehst ehn·deh·<u>reh</u>·soo]
– the airport	**– ao aeroporto** ahoo uh·eh·rau·<u>paur</u>·too
– the train [railway] station	**– à estação dos comboios [trems]** ah ee·stuh·<u>sohm</u> dooz kaum·<u>boy</u>·ooz [trengs]
I'm late.	**Estou atrasado** ♂ **/atrasada** ♀. ee·<u>stawoo</u> uh·truh·<u>zah</u>·thoo ♂ /uh·truh·<u>zah</u>·thuh ♀

Can you drive *faster/ slower*?	**Pode guiar mais *rapido/devagar*?** pawd gee·<u>ahr</u> meyez <u>*rrah*</u>·*pee·thoo/deh·vuh·<u>gahr</u>*
Stop/Wait here.	***Pare/Espere* aqui.** *pah·reh/ee·<u>speh</u>·reh* uh·<u>kee</u>
How much?	**Quanto é?** <u>kwuhn</u>·too eh
You said it would cost…*euros/reais*.	**Disse que ia custar…*euros/reais*.** <u>thee</u>·seh keh <u>ee</u>·uh koo·<u>stahr</u>…*<u>ehoo</u>·rooz/rree·<u>eyez</u>*
A receipt, please.	**Um recibo, se faz favor.** oong reh·<u>see</u>·boo seh fahz fuh·<u>vaur</u>
Keep the change.	**Guarde o troco.** goo·<u>ahr</u>·deh oo <u>trau</u>·koo

You May Hear…

Para donde? <u>puh</u>·ruh <u>thaun</u>·deh	Where to?
Qual é a direção? kwahl eh uh dee·reh·<u>sohm</u>	What's the address?

i Taxis in Portugal are cream colored or black with a green roof. Rural taxis, including those at airports, are marked "A" (**aluguer**) and are usually without a meter, but follow a standard-fare table. They are easily hailed in much of Lisbon, and fares are generally cheap.

All Brazilian taxis have meters, except in small towns, where the fare should be agreed to in advance.

Tipping suggestions: 10% in Portugal and R$ 0.20–0.90 in Brazil.

Car

Car Rental [Hire]

Where can I rent a car?	**Onde posso alugar um carro?** aund <u>paw</u>·soo uh·loo·<u>gahr</u> oong <u>kah</u>·rroo
I'd like to rent…	**Queria alugar…** keh·<u>ree</u>·uh uh·loo·<u>gahr</u>…
– a *2-/4*-door car	**– um carro de *duas/quatro* portas** oong <u>kah</u>·rroo deh *<u>thoo</u>·uhz/<u>kwah</u>·troo* pawr·tuhz

– a(n) *automatic/ manual*	– **um carro *automatico/ de mudanças*** oong <u>kah</u>•rroo *awoo•too•<u>mah</u>•tee•kool deh moo•<u>thuhn</u>•suhz*
– a car with air conditioning	– **um carro com ar condicionado** oong <u>kah</u>•rroo kaum ahr kawn•<u>dee</u>•seeoo•<u>nah</u>•thoo
– a car seat	– **um assento de carro de bebê** oong uh•<u>sehn</u>•too deh <u>kah</u>•rroo deh beh•<u>beh</u>
How much...	**Quanto é...?** <u>kwuhn</u>•too eh...
– per *day/week*	– **por *dia/semana*** poor <u>dee</u>•uh/seh•<u>muh</u>•nuh
– per kilometer	– **por quilómetro** poor kee•<u>law</u>•meh•troo
– for unlimited mileage	– **por milhagem ilimitados** mee•<u>lyah</u>•zseng ee•lee•mee•<u>tah</u>•thooz
– with insurance	– **com seguro** kaum seh•<u>goo</u>•roo
Are there any discounts?	**Há descontos?** ah dehs•<u>kaum</u>•tooz

You May Hear...

Tem uma carta de conduzir internacional? teng <u>oo</u>•muh <u>kahr</u>•tuh deh kaum•doo•<u>zeer</u> een•tehr•nuh•see•oo•<u>nahl</u>	Do you have an international driver's license?
O seu passaporte, por favor. oo sehoo pah•suh•<u>pawr</u>•teh poor fuh•<u>vaur</u>	Your passport, please.
Quer seguro? kehr seh•<u>goo</u>•roo	Do you want insurance?
É preciso deixar um sinal de... eh preh•<u>see</u>•zoo day•<u>shahr</u> oong see•<u>nahl</u> deh...	There is a deposit of...
Assine aqui, se faz favor. uh•<u>see</u>•neh uh•<u>kee</u> seh fahz fuh•<u>vaur</u>	Please sign here.

35

Gas [Petrol] Station

Where's the next gas [petrol] station?	**Onde é a bomba de gasolina [o posto] mais próxima [próximo]?** aund eh uh <u>baum</u>·buh deh guh·zoo·<u>lee</u>·nuh [oo <u>paws</u>·too] meyez <u>praw</u>·see·muh [praw·see·moo]
Fill it up, please.	**Enche o depósito [tanque], se faz favor.** <u>ehn</u>·sheh oo deh·<u>paw</u>·zee·too [<u>tuhn</u>·keh] seh fahz fuh·<u>vaur</u>
...liters, please.	**...litros, se faz favor.** ...<u>lee</u>·trooz seh fahz fuh·<u>vaur</u>
I'll pay *in cash/by credit card.*	**Pago *a dinheiro/com o cartão de crédito.*** <u>pah</u>·goo *uh dee·<u>nyay</u>·roo/kaum oo kuhr·<u>tohm</u> deh <u>kreh</u>·dee·too*

You May See...

NORMAL	regular
SUPER	premium [super]
GASÓLEO [DIESEL]	diesel

Asking Directions

Is this the right road to...?	**Esta é a estrada que vai para...?** <u>eh</u>·stuh eh uh ee·<u>strah</u>·duh keh veye <u>puh</u>·ruh...
How far is it to...?	**A que distância fica...?** uh keh dee·<u>stuhn</u>·see·uh <u>fee</u>·kuh...
Where's...?	**Onde fica...?** aund <u>fee</u>·kuh...
– ...Street	**– Rua...** <u>rroo</u>·uh...

– this address	– **esta morada [neste endereço]** eh·stuh maw·<u>rah</u>·duh [nehst ehn·deh·<u>reh</u>·soo]
– the highway [motorway]	– **a auto-estrada** uh <u>ahoo</u>·taw·<u>strah</u>·duh
Can you show me on the map?	**Pode-me indicar no mapa?** pawd meh een·dee·<u>kahr</u> noo <u>mah</u>·puh
I'm lost.	**Estou perdido** ♂**/perdida** ♀. ee·<u>stawoo</u> pehr·<u>dee</u>·doo ♂/pehr·<u>dee</u>·duh ♀

You May Hear…

sempre em frente <u>sehm</u>·preh eng <u>frehn</u>·teh	straight ahead
à esquerda ah ee·<u>skehr</u>·duh	on the left
à direita ah dee·<u>ray</u>·tuh	on the right
à/ ao **dobrar da esquina** *ah/ahoo* doo·<u>brahr</u> duh ees·<u>kee</u>·nuh	*on/around* the corner
em frente de eng <u>frehn</u>·teh deh	opposite
por trás de poor trahz deh	behind
a seguir a ♀**/o** ♂ uh seh·<u>geer</u> uh♂/oo♀	next to
depois do ♂**/da** ♀ deh·<u>poyz</u> thoo♂/duh♀	after
norte/sul nawrt/sool	north/south
deste/oeste <u>dehs</u>·the/aw·<u>ehs</u>·teh	east/west
no semáforo noo seh·<u>mah</u>·fau·roo	at the traffic light
no cruzamento noo croo·zuh·<u>mehn</u>·too	at the intersection

You May See...

Road Signs in Portugal are "universal," that is, there is no language associated with them. Here are the most common signs with the English explanation below them:

	proibida ultrapassar	do not pass
	sintido proibido	no entry
	estacionamento proibido	no parking
(50)	speed limite	speed limit
STOP	paragem obrigatoria	stop
	finale de facha rodagem	lane ends
	dar prioridade	yield

i A word of caution: Outside of Lisbon, Portugal is mostly mountainous terrain with small, narrow, two-way streets. Overtaking slow moving traffic on the left is permissible, but use caution. At night, when on these unlit winding roads, flash your high beams before every turn to let any oncoming cars on the opposite side know that there's a car around the bend

Parking

Can I park here?

Posso estacionar aqui? paw·soo ee·stuh·seeoo·<u>nahr</u> uh·<u>kee</u>

Where is the nearest parking garage/ parking lot [car park]?	**Onde fica *a garagem mais próxima/um parque de estacionamento mais próximo*?** aund fee·kuh uh guh·*rah*·zseng meyez *praw*·see·muh/oong *pahr*·keh deh ee·stuh·seeawn·uh·*mehn*·too meyez *praw*·see·moo
How much?	**Quanto é…?** *kwuhn*·too eh…
– per hour	**– por hora** poor *aw*·ruh
– per day	**– por dia** poor *dee*·uh
– overnight	**– só uma noite** saw *oo*·muh noyt

In Portugal, metered parking is common in most towns. During business hours there is a 90-minute parking limit; stick to it or you can get fined. Certain cities have blue zones—streets marked with blue-colored signs where you can pay to park. A ticket machine is usually located in the middle of the block and accepts parking tokens. These parking tokens are available from the police or the Portuguese Motoring Organization (ACP). To park in this zone, purchase a ticket and display it in your windshield.

In Brazil, permits may be sold by traffic wardens or at street stalls. The use of parking lots is advisable in Brazilan cities to avoid parking fines or car theft, and offers to "look after" your car.

Breakdown and Repairs

My car *broke down/ won't start*.	**Meu carro quebrou./O motor não pega.** mehoo *kah*·rroo keh·*brawoo*/oo moo·*taur* nohm *peh*·guh
Can you fix it (today)?	**Pode consertá-lo (hoje)?** pawd kaum·sehr·*tah*·loo (oyzseh)
When will it be ready?	**Quando estará pronto?** *kwuhn*·doo ee·stuh·*rah* *praun*·too
How much is it?	**Quanto custa?** *kwuhn*·too *koo*·stuh

Accidents

There has been an accident.
Houve um acidente. auoov oong uh·see·<u>dehnt</u>

Call *an ambulance/ the police.*
Chame *uma ambulância/a polícia.* shuh·meh <u>oo</u>·muh uhm·boo·<u>luhn</u>·see·uh/uh poo·<u>lee</u>·see·uh

Accommodations

Essential

Can you recommend a hotel?
Pode recomendar-me um hotel? pawd reh·kaw·mehn·<u>dahr</u>·meh oong aw·<u>tehl</u>

I have a reservation.
Tenho uma reserva. <u>teh</u>·nyoo <u>oo</u>·muh reh·<u>zehr</u>·vuh

My name is...
Chamo-me... [Meu nome é...] shuh·moo·meh... [mehoo <u>naum</u>·eh eh...]

Do you have a room...?
Tem um quarto...? teng oong <u>kwahr</u>·too...

– for *one/two*
– **para *um/dois*** <u>puh</u>·ruh *oong/doyz*

– with a bathroom
– **com quarto de banho** kaum <u>kwahr</u>·too deh <u>buh</u>·nyoo

– with air conditioning
– **com ar condicionado** kaum ar kawn·dee·seeoo·<u>nah</u>·thoo

For...
Para... <u>puh</u>·ruh...

– tonight
– **hoje à noite** auzseh <u>ah</u> noyt

– two nights
– **duas noites** <u>thoo</u>·uhz noytz

– one week
– **uma semana** <u>oo</u>·muh seh·<u>muh</u>·nuh

How much is it?
Quanto custa? <u>kwuhn</u>·too <u>koo</u>·stuh

Do you have anything cheaper?
Há mais barato? ah meyez buh·<u>rah</u>·too

What time is check-out?	**A que horas temos de deixar o quarto?** uh kee <u>aw</u>·ruhz <u>teh</u>·mooz deh thay·<u>shahr</u> oo <u>kwahr</u>·too
Can I leave this in the safe?	**Posso deixar isto no cofre?** <u>paw</u>·soo thay·<u>shahr</u> ee·stoo noo <u>kaw</u>·freh
Can I leave my bags?	**Posso deixar a minha bagagem?** <u>paw</u>·soo day·<u>shahr</u> uh <u>mee</u>·nyuh buh·<u>gah</u>·geng
Can I have *the bill/ a receipt*?	**Pode dar-me *a conta/uma factura [um recibo]*?** pawd <u>dahr</u>·meh uh <u>kaum</u>·tuh/<u>oo</u>·muh fah·<u>too</u>·ruh [oong reh·<u>see</u>·boo]
I'll pay *in cash/by credit card*.	**Pago *a dinheiro/com o cartão de crédito*.** <u>pah</u>·goo uh dee·<u>nyay</u>·roo/kaum oo kuhr·<u>tohm</u> deh <u>kreh</u>·dee·too

Finding Lodging

Can you recommend a hotel?	**Pode recomendar-me um hotel?** pawd reh·kaw·mehn·<u>dahr</u>·meh oong aw·<u>tehl</u>
What is it near?	**É perto de o que?** eh <u>pehr</u>·too deh oo keh
How do I get there?	**Como se vai para lá?** <u>kau</u>·moo seh veye <u>puh</u>·ruh lah

41

All types of accommodations can be found through the **Oficina de Turismo** (Tourist Information Center).

In Portugal **Turismo no Espaço Rural** offers privately owned homes ranging from manor houses (**Turismo de Habitação**) to country houses in rural settings (**Turismo Rural**) and farmhouses (**Agro-tourism**). In the Algarve and other seaside resorts, you should have little trouble finding locals wanting to rent a room in their own house.

In Brazil, the cheapest form of accommodations is the **dormitório**, providing a shared room for a few reais per night. Other kinds of lodging are:

Hotel
Hotels in Portugal are graded from 2-star to 5-star deluxe; in Brazil, where most hotels are regulated by **Embratur** (the Brazilian Toruism Authority) there are five official categories.

Hotel-Apartamento
Apartment hotels ranging from 2- to 4-star.

Hotel fazenda
Farmhouse lodges, generally equipped with a swimming pool, tennis court and horseback-riding facilities.

Pousada
A state-owned inn converted from an old castle, monastery, convent, palace or in a location of interest to tourists.

Pensão
Corresponds to a boarding house. Usually divided into four categories.

Pousada de juventude
Youth hostel; there are nearly 20 in Portugal and over 90 in Brazil. In Brazil, hostels are open to anyone, though members obtain discounts.

Residencial
Bed and breakfast accommodations.

At the Hotel

I have a reservation.	**Tenho uma reserva.** teh-nyoo oo-muh reh-zehr-vuh
My name is…	**Chamo-me… [Meu nome é…]** shuh-moo meh… [mehoo naum-ee eh…]
Do you have a room…?	**Tem um quarto…?** teng oong kwahr-too…
– with a *bathroom [toilet]/shower*	– **com *banho/chuveiro*** kaum *buh-nyoo/ shoo-vay-roo*
– with air conditioning	– **com ar condicionado** kaum ar kawn-dee-seeoo-nah-thoo
– that's *smoking/ non-smoking*	– **para *fumadores* [*fumantes*]/ *não-fumadores* [*não-fumantes*]** puh-ruh *foo-muh-daurz* [*foo-muhnts*]/*nohm foo-muh-daurz* [*nohm foo-muhnts*]
For…	**Para…** puh-ruh…
– tonight	– **hoje à noite** auzseh ah noyt
– two nights	– **duas noites** thoo-uhz noytz
– one week	– **uma semana** oo-muh seh-muh-nuh

▶ For numbers, see page 177.

Does the hotel have…?	**O hotel tem…?** oo aw-tehl teng…
– a computer	– **um computador** oong kaum-poo-tuh-daur
– an elevator [lift]	– **um elevador** oong eh-leh-vuh-daur
– (wireless) internet service	– **serviço de internet (de rádio)** sehr-vee-soo deh een-tehr-neht (deh rah-dee-oo)
– room service	– **serviço de quartos** sehr-vee-soo deh kwahr-tooz
– a pool	– **piscina** pee-see-nuh
– a gym	– **um ginásio** oong zsee-nah-zee-oo

I need…	**Preciso de…** preh·*see*·zoo deh…
– an extra bed	– **outra cama** auoo·truh *kuh*·muh
– a cot	– **cama de lona** *kuh*·muh deh *law*·nuh
– a crib [child's cot]	– **uma cama de bebé [nenê]** oo·muh *kuh*·muh de beh·*beh* [neh·*neh*]

You May Hear…

O seu *passaporte/cartão de crédito*, por favor. oo sehoo *pah·suh·pawrt*/kuhr·*tohm* deh *kreh·dee·too* poor fuh·*vaur*	Your *passport/credit card*, please.
Preencha esta ficha, por favor. pree·*ehn*·shuh eh·stuh *fee*·shuh poor fuh·*vaur*	Please fill out this form.
Assine aqui. uh·*see*·neh uh·*kee*	Sign here.

Price

How much per *night/week*?	**Quanto é por *noite/semana*?** *kwuhn*·too eh poor noyt/seh·*muh*·nuh
Does the price include *breakfast/sales tax*?	**O preço inclui *o pequeno almoço/taxa*?** oo *preh*·soo een·*kloo*·ee oo peh·*keh*·noo ahl·*mau*·soo/*tah*·shuh

Questions

Where's…?	**Onde é…?** aund eh…
– the bar	– **o bar** oo bar
– the bathroom [toilet]	– **a casa de banho [o banheiro]** uh *kah*·zuh deh *buh*·nyoo [oo buh·*nyay*·roo]
– the elevator [lift]	– **o elevador** oo eh·leh·vuh·*daur*

44

Can I have…?	**Pode arranjar-me [arrumar-me]…?** pawd uh·rrehn·<u>zsahr</u>·meh [ah·rroo·<u>mahr</u>·me]…
– a blanket	**– um cobertor** oong koo·behr·<u>taur</u>
– an iron	**– um ferro de engomar** oong <u>feh</u>·rroo deh ehn·goo·<u>mahr</u>
– a pillow	**– uma almofada [um travesseiro]** <u>oo</u>·muh ahl·moo·<u>fah</u>·duh [oong truh·veh·<u>say</u>·roo]
– soap	**– um sabonete** oong suh·boo·<u>neht</u>
– toilet paper	**– papel higiénico** puh·<u>pehl</u> ee·<u>zseh</u>·nee·koo
– a towel	**– uma toalha** <u>oo</u>·muh too·<u>ah</u>·lyuh
Do you have an adapter for this?	**Tem um adaptador para isto?** teng oong uh·duhp·tuh·<u>daur</u> puh·ruh ee·stoo
How do I turn on the lights?	**Como é que se acende as luzes?** <u>kau</u>·moo eh keh seh uh·<u>sehn</u>·deh uhz <u>loo</u>·zehz
Could you wake me at…?	**Podia acordar-me às…?** poo·<u>dee</u>·uh uh·koor·<u>dahr</u>·meh ahz…
Can I leave this in the safe?	**Posso deixar isto no cofre?** <u>paw</u>·soo thay·<u>shahr</u> ee·stoo noo <u>kaw</u>·freh
I'd like to get my things from the safe.	**Queria tirar as minhas coisas do cofre.** keh·<u>ree</u>·uh tee·<u>rahr</u> uhz <u>mee</u>·nyuhz <u>koy</u>·zuhz thoo <u>kaw</u>·freh
Is/Are there any *mail/ messages* for me?	**Há *correio [correspondência]/ alguma mensagem* para mim?** ah koo·<u>rray</u>·oo [kaw·rrehs·paun·<u>dehn</u>·see·uh]/ahl·<u>goo</u>·muh mehn·<u>sah</u>·zseng puh·ruh meeng

Restrooms in Portugal are labeled W.C. Major cities have public toilets that are automatically sanitized after each use. They are found on the street and have a small fee per use. Some of these public restrooms have 20-minute time limits, and the door will automatically open when your time is up.

In hotels and private residences, it is standard for bathrooms to be equipped with bidets.

You May See...

EMPURRAR/PUXAR	push/pull
CASA DE BANHO [O BANHEIRO]/LAVAROS	bathroom/restroom [toilet]
CHUVEIRO	shower
ELEVADOR	elevator [lift]
ESCADAS	stairs
LAVANDERIA	laundry
NÃO PERTURBAR	do not disturb
PORTA DE INCÊNDIO	fire door
SAÍDA (DE EMERGÊNCIA)	(emergency) exit
CHAMADA PARA DESPERTAR	wake-up call

Problems

There's a problem. **Há um problema.** ah oong proo·bleh·muh

I've lost my *key/key card*. **Perdi a minha *chave/carta de chave*.** pehr·dee uh mee·nyuh shahv/kahr·tuh deh shahv

I've locked myself out of my room. **Fechei-me fora do quarto.** fee·shay·meh faw·ruh thoo kwahr·too

There's no *hot water/toilet paper*. **Não há *água quente/papel higiénico*.** nohm ah ah·gwuh kehnt/puh·pehl ee·zseh·nee·koo

The room is dirty. **O quarto está sujo.** oo kwahr·too ee·stah soo·zsoo

There are bugs in our room. **Há insectos no quarto.** ah een·sehk·tooz noo kwahr·too

...doesn't work. **...tem um defeito.** ...teng oong deh·fay·too

Can you fix...? **Pode arranjar...?** pawd uh·rrehn·zsahr...

46

– the air conditioning	**– o ar condicionado** oo ar kawn·dee·seeoo·<u>nah</u>·thoo
– the fan	**– a ventoinha [o ventilador]** uh vehn·too·<u>ee</u>·nyuh [oo vehn·tee·luh·<u>daur</u>]
– the heat [heating]	**– o aquecimento** oo uh·keh·see·<u>mehn</u>·too
– the lights	**– as luzes** uhz <u>loo</u>·zehz
– the TV	**– a TV** uh teh·<u>veh</u>
– the toilet	**– a retrete** uh reh·<u>treht</u>
I'd like to move to another room.	**Queria mudar de quarto.** keh·<u>ree</u>·uh moo·<u>dahr</u> deh <u>kwahr</u>·too

i The 220-volt, 50-cycle AC is the norm throughout Portugal. If you bring your own electrical appliances, buy an adapter plug (round pins, not square) before leaving home. The electrical current in Brazil is not completely standardized. Some parts of Brazil are 220 V while others are 110 V. Most of Brazil, including Rio de Janeiro and São Paulo, is 110 or 120 V, 60 Hz AC.

Check-out

When's check-out?	**A que horas temos de deixar o quarto?** uh kee <u>aw</u>·ruhz <u>teh</u>·mooz deh thay·<u>shahr</u> oo <u>kwahr</u>·too
Could I leave my bags here until…?	**Posso deixar a minha bagagem aqui até…?** <u>paw</u>·soo day·<u>shahr</u> uh <u>mee</u>·nyuh buh·<u>gah</u>·zseng uh·<u>kee</u> uh·<u>teh</u>…
Can I have *an itemized bill/a receipt*?	**Pode dar-me *uma conta detalhada/uma factura* [*um recibo*]?** pawd <u>dahr</u>·meh <u>oo</u>·muh <u>kaum</u>·tuh deh·tuh·<u>lyah</u>·duh/<u>oo</u>·muh fah·<u>too</u>·ruh [oong reh·<u>see</u>·boo]
I think there's a mistake.	**Creio que se enganou.** <u>kray</u>·oo keh seh ehn·guh·<u>nau</u>
I'll pay *in cash/by credit card*.	**Pago *a dinheiro/com o cartão de crédito*.** <u>pah</u>·goo uh dee·<u>nyay</u>·roo/kaum oo <u>kuhr</u>·tohm deh <u>kreh</u>·dee·too

Renting

I reserved *an apartment/a room*.	**Reservei um *apartamento/quarto*.** reh·zehr·<u>vay</u> oong uh·puhr·tuh·<u>mehn</u>·too/<u>kwahr</u>·too
My name is…	**Chamo-me… [Meu nome é…]** <u>shuh</u>·moo meh… [mehoo <u>naum</u>·ee eh…]
Can I have the *key/key card*?	**Posso ter a *chave/carta de chave*?** <u>paw</u>·soo tehr uh *shahv/<u>kahr</u>·tuh deh shahv*
Are there…?	**Há…?** ah…
– dishes [crockery]	**– a louça** uh <u>lau</u>·suh
– pillows	**– almofadas** ahl·moo·<u>fah</u>·duhz
– sheets	**– lençóis** lehn·<u>soyz</u>
– towels	**– toalhas** too·<u>ah</u>·lyuhz
– utensils [cutlery]	**– os talheres** ooz tuh·<u>lyeh</u>·rehz
When do I put out the *trash [rubbish]/recycling*?	**Quando ponho o *lixo/reciclar* lá fora?** <u>kwuhn</u>·doo <u>paw</u>·nyoo oo *<u>lee</u>·shoo/ree·see·<u>klahr</u>* lah <u>faw</u>·ruh
…is broken.	**…está partido ♂/partida ♀ [quebrado ♂/quebrada ♀].** …ee·<u>stah</u> puhr·<u>tee</u>·thoo ♂/ puhr·<u>tee</u>·thuh ♀ [keh·<u>brah</u>·doo ♂/ keh·<u>brah</u>·duh ♀]

48

How does…work?	**Como funciona…?** <u>kau</u>·moo faun·see·<u>aw</u>·nuh…
– the air conditioner	**– o ar condicionado** oo ar kawn·dee·seeoo·<u>nah</u>·thoo
– the dishwasher	**– a machina de lavar pratos** uh <u>mah</u>·kee·nuh deh luh·<u>vahr</u> <u>prah</u>·tooz
– the freezer	**– a arca frigorífica [o congelador]** uh <u>ahr</u>·kuh free·goo·<u>ree</u>·fee·kuh [oo kaum·zseh·luh·<u>daur</u>]
– the heater	**– o aquecedor** oo uh·<u>keh</u>·seh·daur
– the microwave	**– o microondas** oo mee·krau·<u>aun</u>·duhz
– the refrigerator	**– o frigorífico [a geladeira]** oo free·goo·<u>ree</u>·fee·koo [uh zseh·luh·<u>thay</u>·ruh]
– the stove	**– o fogão** oo foo·<u>gohm</u>
– the washing machine	**– a máquina de lavar (roupa)** uh <u>mah</u>·kee·nuh deh luh·<u>vahr</u> (<u>rauoo</u>·puh)

Household Items

I need…	**Preciso de…** preh·<u>see</u>·zoo deh…
– an adapter	**– um adaptador** oong uh·duhp·tuh·<u>daur</u>
– aluminum [kitchen] foil	**– papel de alumínio** puh·<u>pehl</u> deh uh·loo·<u>mee</u>·nee·oo
– a bottle opener	**– um abre-garrafas [abridor de garrafas]** oong ah·breh·guh·<u>rrah</u>·fuhz [uh·bree·<u>daur</u> deh guh·<u>rrah</u>·fuhz]
– a broom	**– uma vassoura** <u>oo</u>·muh vuh·<u>sau</u>·ruh
– a can opener	**– um abre-latas [abridor de latas]** oong ah·breh·<u>lah</u>·tuhz [ah·bree·<u>daur</u> deh <u>lah</u>·tuhz]
– cleaning supplies	**– produtos de limpeza** prau·<u>thoo</u>·tooz deh leem·<u>peh</u>·zuh
– a corkscrew	**– um saca-rolhas** oong sah·kuh·<u>rau</u>·lyuz

I need...	Preciso de... preh-<u>see</u>-zoo deh...
– detergent	– **detergente em pó para a roupa** deh-tehr-<u>zsehnt</u> eng paw <u>puh</u>-ruh uh <u>rauoo</u>-puh
– dishwashing liquid	– **detergente para a louça** deh-tehr-<u>zsehnt</u> <u>puh</u>-ruh uh <u>lau</u>-suh
– garbage [rubbish] bags	– **sacos para o lixo** <u>sah</u>-kooz <u>puh</u>-ruh oo <u>lee</u>-shoo
– a light bulb	– **uma lâmpada eléctrica** <u>oo</u>-muh <u>luhm</u>-puh-duh ee-<u>leh</u>-tree-kuh
– matches	– **fósforos** <u>fawz</u>-fuh-rooz
– a mop	– **o esfregão** oo ees-fruh-<u>gohm</u>
– paper napkins	– **guardanapos de papel** gwahr-duh-<u>nah</u>-pooz deh puh-<u>pehl</u>
– paper towels	– **papel da cozinha** puh-<u>pehl</u> duh koo-<u>zee</u>-nyuh
– plastic wrap [cling film]	– **papel aderente** puh-<u>pehl</u> uh-deh-<u>rehnt</u>
– a plunger	– **um desentupidor** oong deh-zehn-too-pee-<u>daur</u>
– scissors	– **uma tesoura** <u>oo</u>-muh teh-<u>zau</u>-ruh
– a vacuum cleaner	– **um aspirador** oong uh-spee-ruh-<u>daur</u>

▶ For dishes, utensils and kitchen tools, see page 71.

▶ For oven temperatures, see page 185.

Hostel

Do you have any places left for tonight?	**Ainda há vagas para hoje à noite?** uh-<u>een</u>-duh ah <u>vah</u>-guhz <u>puh</u>-ruh auzseh <u>ah</u> noyt
Can I have...?	**Pode dar-me...?** pawd <u>dahr</u>-meh...
– a *single/double* room	– **um quarto *individual/duplo*** oong <u>kwahr</u>-too een-dee-vee-doo-<u>ahl</u>/<u>doo</u>-ploo

– a blanket	**– um cobertor** oong koo·behr·<u>taur</u>
– a pillow	**– uma almofada [um travesseiro]** <u>oo</u>·muh ahl·moo·<u>fah</u>·duh [oong truh·veh·<u>say</u>·roo]
– sheets	**– lençóis** lehn·<u>soyz</u>
– a towel	**– uma toalha** <u>oo</u>·muh too·<u>ah</u>·lyuh
What time are the doors locked?	**A que horas fecham as portas?** uh keh <u>aw</u>·ruhz feh·<u>shohm</u> uhz <u>pawr</u>·tuhz

> *i* There are nearly twenty youth hostels in Portugal and over ninety in Brazil. In Portugal, prices for a room at a hostel range anywhere from seventeen to sixty-five euros. In order to stay in a hostel in Portugal, you must be under the age of twenty-six and have a Youth Card. If you do not have a Youth Card, you can purchase one at the hostel upon arrival. The Youth Card is valid until your twenty-sixth birthday. In Brazil, hostels are open to anyone, though members who have a Youth Card receive discounts.

Camping

Can I camp here?	**Posso acampar aqui?** <u>paw</u>·soo uh·kuhm·<u>pahr</u> uh·<u>kee</u>
Where's the campsite?	**Onde é o parque de campismo [camping]?** aund eh oo <u>pahr</u>·keh deh kuhm·<u>peez</u>·moo [<u>kuhm</u>·peeng]
What is the charge per *day/week*?	**Qual é a tarifa por *dia/semana*?** kwahl eh uh tuh·<u>ree</u>·fuh poor *<u>dee</u>·uh/seh·<u>muh</u>·nuh*
Are there…?	**Há…?** ah…
– cooking facilities	**– uma área para se cozinhar** <u>oo</u>·muh <u>ah</u>·ree·uh <u>puh</u>·ruh seh koo·zee·<u>nyahr</u>
– electrical outlets	**– electricidade** ee·leh·tree·see·<u>dahd</u>
– laundry facilities	**– uma lavandaria** <u>oo</u>·muh luh·vuhn·deh·<u>ree</u>·uh

Are there…?	**Há…?** ah…
– showers	**– o chuveiro** oo shoo·<u>vay</u>·roo
– tents for rent [hire]	**– tendas para aluguer** <u>tehn</u>·duhz <u>puh</u>·ruh uh·loo·<u>gehr</u>
Where can I empty the chemical toilet?	**Onde posso esvaziar o banheiro químico?** aund <u>paw</u>·soo ees·vee·<u>ahr</u> oo buh·<u>nyay</u>·roo <u>kee</u>·mee·koo

You May See…

ÁGUA POTÁVEL	drinking water
É PROIBIDO ACAMPAR	no camping
É PROIBIDO *ACENDER FOGOS/CHURRASCAR*	no *fires/barbecues*

▶ For household items, see page 49.

▶ For dishes, utensils and kitchen tools, see page 71.

Internet and Communications

Essential

Where's an internet café?	**Onde fica um bar de internet?** aund <u>fee</u>·kuh oong bahr deh een·tehr·<u>neht</u>
Can I access the Internet here?	**Tenho acesso á internet aqui?** <u>teh</u>·nyoo uh·<u>seh</u>·soo ah een·tehr·<u>neht</u> uh·<u>kee</u>
Can I check e-mail here?	**Posso ler o meu e-mail aqui?** <u>paw</u>·soo lehr oo mehoo ee·<u>mehl</u> uh·<u>khee</u>
How much per (half) hour?	**Quanto é por (meia) hora?** <u>kwuhn</u>·too eh poor (<u>may</u>·uh) <u>aw</u>·ruh
How do I *connect/ log on*?	**Como *conecto/logue*?** kau·moo koo·<u>nehk</u>·too/<u>law</u>·geh

52

A phone card, please.	**Um credifone [cartão telefônico], se faz favor.** oong kreh·dee·<u>faun</u> [kuhr·<u>tohm</u> tehl·eh·<u>fawn</u>·ee·koo] seh fahz fuh·<u>vaur</u>
Can I have your phone number?	**Pode dar-me o seu número de telefone?** pawd <u>dahr</u>·meh oo sehoo <u>noo</u>·meh·roo deh tehl·<u>fawn</u>
Here's my *number/e-mail address*.	**Este é o meu *número/e-mail*.** ehst eh oo mehoo <u>noo</u>·meh·roo/ee·<u>mehl</u>
Call me.	**Telefone-me.** tehl·<u>fawn</u>·eh·meh
E-mail me.	**Envie me um e-mail.** ehn·<u>vee</u>·eh meh oong ee·<u>mehl</u>
Hello. This is…	**Estou [Alô]. Fala…** ee·<u>stawoo</u> [aw·<u>lah</u>]. fah·luh…
I'd like to speak to…	**Queria falar com…** keh·<u>ree</u>·uh fuh·<u>lahr</u> kaum…
Could you repeat that, please?	**Importa-se de repetir, por favor?** eem·<u>pawr</u>·tuh·seh deh reh·peh·<u>teer</u> poor fuh·<u>vaur</u>
I'll call back later.	**Chamo mais tarde.** <u>shuh</u>·moo meyez <u>tahr</u>·deh
Bye.	**Adeus.** uh·<u>deeoosh</u>
Where's the post office?	**Onde são os correios?** aund sohm ooz koo·<u>rray</u>·ooz
I'd like to send this to…	**Gostaria de mandar isto para…** goo·stuh·<u>ree</u>·uh deh muhn·<u>dahr</u> ee·stoo <u>puh</u>·ruh…

Computer, Internet and E-mail

Where's an internet cafe?	**Onde fica um bar de internet?** aund <u>fee</u>·kuh oong bahr deh een·tehr·<u>neht</u>
Does it have wireless internet?	**Tem internet de rádio?** teng een·tehr·<u>neht</u> deh <u>rah</u>·dee·oo

How do I turn the computer *on/off*?	**Como *ligo/desligo* o computador?** <u>kau</u>·moo *lee-<u>goo</u>/dehz-<u>lee</u>-goo* oo kaum·poo·tuh·<u>daur</u>
Can I…?	**Posso…?** <u>paw</u>·soo…
– access the internet	– **aceder a internet** uh·seh·<u>dehr</u> uh een·tehr·<u>neht</u>
– check e-mail	– **ler o meu e-mail** lehr oo mehoo ee·<u>mehl</u>
– print	– **impressar** eeng·preh·<u>sahr</u>
How much per (half) hour?	**Quanto é por (meia) hora?** <u>kwuhn</u>·too eh poor (<u>may</u>·uh) <u>aw</u>·ruh
How do I…?	**Como…?** <u>kau</u>·moo…
– connect/disconnect	– **conecto/desconecto** koo·<u>nehk</u>·too/ dehz·koo·nehk·too
– log *on/off*	– **logue/logoff** <u>law</u>·geh/law·<u>gawf</u>
– type this symbol	– **bato este símbolo** <u>bah</u>·too ehst seem·<u>boo</u>·loo
What's your e-mail?	**Qual é o seu e-mail?** kwahl eh oo sehoo ee·<u>mehl</u>
My e-mail is…	**O meu e-mail é…** oo mehoo ee·<u>mehl</u> eh…

You May See...

FECHAR	close
APAGUE	delete
E-MAIL	e-mail
SAÍDA	exit
AJUDA	help
MENSAGEIRO DE INSTANTE	instant messenger
INTERNET	internet
LOGIN	login
(NOVA) MENSAGEM	(new) message
LIGUE/DESLIGUE	on/off
ABRIR	open
IMPRESSAR	print
GUARDAR	save
MANDAR	send
NOME DO USUÁRIO/SENHA	username/password
INTERNET DE RÁDIO	wireless internet

Phone

A *phone card/prepaid phone*, please.
Um *credifone/fone pré-pago*, por favor. oong *kreh·dee·fawn/fawn* preh·*pah*·goo poor fuh·<u>vaur</u>

How much?
Quanto é? <u>kwuhn</u>·too eh

My phone doesn't work here.
O meu telfone não funciona aqui. oo meehoo tehl·<u>fawn</u> nohm foon·<u>seeaw</u>·nuh uh·<u>kee</u>

What's the *area/country* code for...?
O que é o código de *área/país* para...? oo kee eh oo <u>kaw</u>·dee·goo deh *ah·<u>eh</u>·ree·uh/puh·<u>eez</u>* puh·ruh...

What's the number for Information?	**Qual é o número das Informações?** kwahl eh oo <u>noo</u>·meh·roo duhz eeng·foor·muh·<u>soingz</u>
I'd like the number for...	**Queria o número para...** keh·<u>ree</u>·uh oo <u>noo</u>·meh·roo <u>puh</u>·ruh...
Can I have your number?	**Pode dar-me o seu número de telefone?** pawd <u>dahr</u>·meh oo sehoo <u>noo</u>·meh·roo deh tehl·<u>fawn</u>
Here's my number.	**Este é o meu número.** ehst eh oo mehoo <u>noo</u>·meh·roo

▶For numbers, see page 177.

Call me.	**Telefone-me.** tehl·<u>faw</u>·neh·meh
Text me.	**Manda-me uma mensagem de texto.** <u>muhn</u>·duh·meh <u>oo</u>·muh mehn·<u>sah</u>·zseng deh <u>tehk</u>·stoo
I'll call you.	**Vou telefonar-lhe.** voh tehl·foo·<u>nahr</u>·lyeh
I'll text you.	**Mando-te uma mensagem de texto.** <u>muhn</u>·doo·teh <u>oo</u>·muh mehn·<u>sah</u>·zseng deh <u>tehk</u>·stoo

On the Phone

Hello. This is...	**Estou [Alô]. Fala...** <u>ee</u>·stoo [ah·<u>lawoo</u>]. <u>fah</u>·luh...
I'd like to speak to...	**Queria falar com...** keh·<u>ree</u>·uh fuh·<u>lahr</u> kaum...
Extension...	**Extensão...** ehs·tehn·<u>sohm</u>...
Speak *louder/more slowly*, please.	**Fale mais *alto/devagar*, por favor.** <u>fah</u>·leh meyez *<u>ahl</u>·too/deh·vuh·<u>gahr</u>* poor fuh·<u>vaur</u>
Could you repeat that?	**Importa-se de repetir?** eeng·<u>pawr</u>·tuh·seh deh reh·peh·<u>teer</u>
I'll call back later.	**Eu chamo mais tarde.** eeoo <u>shuh</u>·moo meyez tahrd
Bye.	**Adeus.** uh·<u>deeooz</u>

▶For business travel, see page 152.

You May Hear...

Quem fala? keng <u>fah</u>·luh	Who's calling?
Não desligue. nohm dehs·<u>lee</u>·geh	Hold on.
Vou-o ligar agora. <u>vauoo</u>·oo lee·<u>gahr</u> uh·<u>gaw</u>·ruh	I'll put you through.
Lamento, mas *ele/ela* não está. luh·<u>mehn</u>·too muhz ehl/<u>ehl</u>·uh nohm ee·<u>stah</u>	I'm afraid *he's/she's* not in.
***Ele/Ela* nao pode atender o telefone.** *ehl/<u>ehl</u>·uh* nohm pawd uh·tehn·<u>dehr</u> oo tehl·<u>fawn</u>	*He/She* can't come to the phone.
Quer deixar uma mensagem? kehr day·<u>shahr</u> <u>oo</u>·muh mehn·<u>sah</u>·zseng	Would you like to leave a message?
Chame *mais tarde/em dez minutos.* <u>shuh</u>·meh *meyez <u>tahr</u>·deh/eng dehz mee·<u>noo</u>·tooz*	Call back *later/in ten minutes.*
***Ele/Ela* pode telefonar para traz?** *ehl/<u>ehl</u>·uh* pawd tehl·fawn·<u>ahr</u> puh·ruh trahz	Can *he/she* call you back?
Qual é o seu numero de telefone? kwahl eh oo sehoo <u>noo</u>·meh·roo deh tehl·<u>fawn</u>	What's your number?

57

Fax

Can I *send/receive* a fax here?	**Posso *enviar/receber* um fax aqui?** paw·soo *ehn·vee·ahr/reh·seh·behr* oong fahks uh·kee
What's the fax number?	**O que é o número de fax?** oo keh eh oo noo·meh·roo deh fahks
Please fax this to…	**Por favor mande este fax para…** poor fuh·vaur muhn·deh ehst fahks puh·ruh…

Post Office

Where's the *post office/mailbox* [*postbox*]?	**Onde é que é *o correio/a caixa do correio?*** aund eh keh eh oo koo·rray·oo/uh keye·shuh thoo koo·rray·oo
A stamp for this *postcard/letter*, please.	**Um selo para *este postal/esta carta*, se faz favor.** oong seh·loo puh·ruh *ehst poo·stahl/eh·stuh kahr·tuh* seh fahz fuh·vaur
How much?	**Quanto é?** kwuhn·too eh
I want to send this package by *airmail/ express.*	**Queria mandar este embrulho [pacote] por *via aérea/correio expresso.*** keh·ree·uh muhn·dahr eh·stuh ehm·broo·lyoo [puh·kawt] poor *vee·uh uh·eh·ree·uh/koo·rray·oo ees·preh·soo*
A receipt, please.	**Um recibo, se faz favor.** oong reh·see·boo seh fahz fuh·vaur

You May Hear...

Por favor preencha a declaração da alfândega. poor fuh·<u>vaur</u> pree·ehn·<u>shuh</u> uh deh·kluh·ruh·<u>sohm</u> duh uhl·<u>fuhn</u>·dee·guh

Please fill out the customs declaration form.

Qual é o valor? kwahl eh oo vuh·<u>laur</u>

What's the value?

O que é que tem dentro? oo kee eh keh teng <u>dehn</u>·troo

What's inside?

Post offices in Portugal are indicated by signs reading CCT (**Correios e Telecomunicações**). Main offices operate until 10:00 p.m. Mondays through Fridays, and on Saturdays and Sundays until 6:00 p.m. Red mailboxes are for **correio normal** (normal mail) and blue for **correio azul** (express mail). You can make phone calls at the post office; calls are paid for at the end of the conversation. Stamps can be bought here and also at any shop bearing the sign of the red horse.

In Brazil, post offices bear the sign ECT (**Empresa Brasileira de Correios e Telégrafos**); they are generally open from 8:00 a.m. to 6:00 p.m. Mondays through Fridays, and until noon on Saturdays. Street corner mailboxes are yellow.

▼ *Food*

Essential

Can you recommend a good *restaurant/bar*?	**Pode recomendar-me um bom *restaurante/bar*?** pawd reh·kaw·mehn·<u>dahr</u>·meh oong bohng *reh·<u>stahoo</u>·ruhnt /bar*
Is there a(n) *traditional Portuguese/inexpensive* restaurant near here?	**Há um restaurante *portuguese tradicional/barato* perto daqui?** ah oong reh·<u>stahoo</u>·ruhnt *por·too·<u>gehz</u> truh·dee·see·oo·<u>nahl</u>/buh·<u>rah</u>·too* pehr·too duh·<u>kee</u>
A table for…, please.	**Uma mesa para…, se faz favor.** <u>oo</u>·muh <u>meh</u>·zuh <u>puh</u>·ruh…seh fahz fuh·<u>vaur</u>
Could we sit…?	**Podemos sentar-nos…?** poo·<u>deh</u>·mooz sehn·<u>tahr</u>·nooz…
– here/there	**– aqui/ali** uh·<u>kee</u>/uh·<u>lee</u>
– outside	**– lá fora** lah <u>faw</u>·ruh
– in a non-smoking area	**– na área para não-fumadores [não-fumantes]** nuh <u>ah</u>·ree·uh <u>puh</u>·ruh nohm foo·muh·<u>daur</u>·ehs [nohm foo·<u>muhnts</u>]
I'm waiting for someone.	**Estou à espera de alguem.** ee·<u>stawoo</u> ah ee·<u>speh</u>·ruh deh ahl·<u>gehm</u>
Where's the restroom [toilet]?	**Onde são as casas de banho [os banheiros]?** aund sohm uhz <u>kah</u>·zuhz deh <u>buh</u>·nyoo [ooz buh·<u>nyay</u>·rooz]
A menu, please.	**Uma ementa, por favor.** <u>oo</u>·muh ee·<u>mehn</u>·tuh poor fuh·<u>vaur</u>
What do you recommend?	**O que é que me recomenda?** oo keh eh keh meh reh·koo·<u>mehn</u>·duh
I'd like…	**Queria…** keh·<u>ree</u>·uh…

Some more…, please.	**Mais…, se faz favor.** meyez…seh fahz fuh·<u>vaur</u>
Enjoy your meal.	**Bom apetite.** bohng uh·peh·<u>tee</u>·teh
The check [bill], please.	**A conta, por favor.** uh <u>kaum</u>·tuh poor fuh·<u>vaur</u>
Is service included?	**O serviço está incluído?** oo sehr·<u>vee</u>·soo ee·<u>stah</u> een·kloo·<u>ee</u>·thoo
Can I pay by credit card?	**Posso pagar com cartão de crédito?** <u>paw</u>·soo puh·<u>gahr</u> kaum kuhr·<u>tohm</u> deh <u>kreh</u>·dee·too
Could I have a receipt, please?	**Pode darme uma factura [um recibo], por favor?** pawd <u>dahr</u>·meh <u>oo</u>·muh fah·<u>too</u>·ruh [oong reh·<u>see</u>·boo] poor fuh·<u>vaur</u>
Thank you.	**Obrigado** ♂**/Obrigada** ♀. aw·bree·<u>gah</u>·thoo ♂/ aw·bree·<u>gah</u>·thuh ♀

Restaurant Types

Can you recommend…?	**Pode recomendar-me…?** pawd reh·koo·mehn·<u>dahr</u>·meh…
– a restaurant	**– um restaurante** oong reh·stuhoo·<u>ruhnt</u>
– a bar	**– um bar** oong bar
– a cafe	**– um café** oong kuh·<u>feh</u>
– a fast-food place	**– um restaurante de comidas rápidas [uma cadeia de fast food]** oong reh·stuhoo·<u>ruhnt</u> deh koo·<u>mee</u>·duhz <u>rah</u>·pee·duhz [<u>oo</u>·muh kuh·<u>day</u>·uh deh fast food]
– a fish restaurant	**– uma marisqueira [um restaurante de frutos do mar]** <u>oo</u>·muh muh·ree·<u>skay</u>·ruh [oong reh·stuhoo·<u>ruhnt</u> deh <u>froo</u>·tooz doo mahr]

Reservations and Questions

I'd like to reserve a table…	**Queria reservar uma mesa…** keh-<u>ree</u>-uh reh-zehr-<u>vahr</u> <u>oo</u>-muh <u>meh</u>-zuh…
– for two	**– para dois** <u>puh</u>-ruh doyz
– for this evening	**– para hoje à noite** <u>puh</u>-ruh auzseh ah noyt
– for tomorrow at…	**– para amanhã às…** <u>puh</u>-ruh uh-muh-<u>nyuh</u> ahz…
A table for two.	**Uma mesa para dois.** <u>oo</u>-muh <u>meh</u>-zuh <u>puh</u>-ruh doyz
We have a reservation.	**Temos uma reservação.** <u>teh</u>-mooz <u>oo</u>-muh reh-zehr-vuh-<u>sohm</u>
My name is…	**Chamo-me… [Meu nome é…]** <u>shuh</u>-moo-meh… [mehoo <u>naum</u>-ee eh…]
Could we sit…?	**Podemos sentar-nos…?** poo-<u>deh</u>-mooz sehn-<u>tahr</u>-nooz…
– here/there	**– aqui/ali** uh-<u>kee</u>/uh-<u>lee</u>
– outside	**– lá fora** lah <u>faw</u>-ruh
– in a non-smoking area	**– na área para não-fumadores [não-fumantes]** nuh <u>ah</u>-ree-uh <u>puh</u>-ruh nohm foo-muh-<u>daur</u>-ehs [nohm foo-<u>muhnts</u>]
– by the window	**– à janela** ah zsuh-<u>neh</u>-luh

Where are the restrooms [toilets]?	**Onde são as casas de banho [os banheiros]?** aund sohm uhz <u>kah</u>·zuhz deh <u>buh</u>·nyoo [ooz buh·<u>nyay</u>·rooz]

Ordering

Excuse me!	**Se faz favor!** seh fahz fuh·<u>vaur</u>
We're ready to order.	**Estamos prontos para encomendar.** ee·<u>stuh</u>·mooz <u>prawn</u>·tooz <u>puh</u>·ruh eng·kau·mehn·<u>dahr</u>
The wine list, please.	**A carta dos vinhos, se faz favor.** uh <u>kahr</u>·tuh dooz <u>vee</u>·nyooz seh fahz fuh·<u>vaur</u>
I'd like...	**Queria...** keh·<u>ree</u>·uh...
– a bottle of...	**– uma garrafa...** <u>oo</u>·muh guh·<u>rrah</u>·fuh...
– a carafe of...	**– um jarro de...** oom <u>jah</u>·rroo deh...
– a glass of...	**– um copo de...** oong <u>kaw</u>·poo deh...

▶ For alcoholic and nonalcoholic drinks, see page 84.

A menu, please.	**Uma ementa, por favor.** oo·muh ee·<u>mehn</u>·tuh poor fuh·<u>vaur</u>
Do you have…?	**Tem…?** teng…
– a menu in English	– **uma ementa em Inglês** oo·muh ee·<u>mehn</u>·tuh eng een·<u>glehz</u>
– a fixed-price menu	– **uma ementa de preço-fixou** oo·muh ee·<u>mehn</u>·tuh deh <u>preh</u>·soo <u>feek</u>·soo
– a children's menu	– **uma ementa de criança** oo·muh ee·<u>mehn</u>·tuh deh kree·<u>uhn</u>·suh
What do you recommend?	**O que é que me recomenda?** oo kee eh keh meh reh·koo·<u>mehn</u>·duh
What's this?	**O que é isto?** oo kee eh <u>ee</u>·stoo
What's in it?	**Leva o quê?** <u>leh</u>·vuh oo keh
Is it spicy?	**É picante?** eh pee·<u>kuhnt</u>
It's to go [take away].	**É para levar.** eh <u>puh</u>·ruh leh·<u>vahr</u>

You May See…

COUVERT	cover charge
PREÇO-FIXO	fixed-price
EMENTA	menu
UMA EMENTA DO DIA	menu of the day
SERVIÇO (NÃO) INCLUÍDO	service (not) included
SPECIAIS	specials

Cooking Methods

baked	**alourado** ♂/**alourada** ♀ [**dourado** ♂/ **dourada** ♀] uh·lauoo·<u>rah</u>·thoo ♂/ uh·lauoo·<u>rah</u>·thuh ♀ [dauoo·<u>rah</u>·doo ♂/ dauoo·<u>rah</u>·duh ♀]

boiled	**cozido** ♂/**cozida** ♀ koo·<u>zee</u>·thoo ♂/ koo·<u>zee</u>·thuh ♀
braised	**estufado** ♂/**estufada** ♀ ee·stoo·<u>fah</u>·thoo ♂/ ee·stoo·<u>fah</u>·thuh ♀
breaded	**panado** ♂/**panada** ♀ **[empanado** ♂/ **empanada** ♀] puh·<u>nah</u>·thoo ♂/puh·<u>nah</u>·thuh ♀ [ehm·puh·<u>nah</u>·doo ♂/ehm·puh·<u>nah</u>·dah ♀]
creamed	**com natas** kohng <u>nah</u>·tuhz
diced	**aos cubos** ahooz <u>koo</u>·booz
fileted	**filete de...** fee·<u>leht</u> deh…
fried	**frito** ♂/**frita** ♀ <u>free</u>·too ♂/<u>free</u>·tuh ♀
grilled	**grelhado** ♂/**grelhada** ♀ gree·<u>lyah</u>·thoo ♂/ gree·<u>lyah</u>·thuh ♀
poached	**escalfado** ♂/**escalfada** ♀ ees·kahl·<u>fah</u>·thoo ♂/ ees·kahl·<u>fah</u>·thuh ♀
roasted	**assado** ♂/**assada** ♀ uh·<u>sah</u>·thoo ♂/ uh·<u>sah</u>·thuh ♀
sautéed	**salteado** ♂/**salteada** ♀ sahl·tee·<u>ah</u>·thoo ♂/ sahl·tee·<u>ah</u>·thuh ♀
smoked	**fumado** ♂/**fumada** ♀ **[defumado** ♂/ **defumada** ♀] foo·<u>mah</u>·thoo ♂/foo·<u>mah</u>·thuh ♀ [deh·foo·<u>mah</u>·doo ♂/deh·foo·<u>mah</u>·duh ♀]
steamed	**cozido** ♂/**cozida** ♀ **a vapor** koo·<u>zee</u>·thoo ♂/ koo·<u>zee</u>·thuh ♀ uh vuh·<u>paur</u>
stewed	**guisado** ♂/**guisada** ♀ **[ensopado** ♂/ **ensopada** ♀] gee·<u>zah</u>·thoo ♂/gee·<u>zah</u>·thuh ♀ [een·soo·<u>pah</u>·doo ♂/een·soo·<u>pah</u>·duh ♀]
stuffed	**recheado** ♂/**recheada** ♀ reh·shee·<u>ah</u>·thoo ♂/ reh·shee·<u>ah</u>·thuh ♀

Special Requirements

I am…	**Sou…** sauoo…
– diabetic	**– diabético ♂/diabética ♀** dee·uh·<u>beh</u>·tee·koo ♂/dee·uh·<u>beh</u>·tee·kuh ♀
– lactose intolerant	**– lactose intolerante** <u>lahk</u>·tawz een·<u>tawl</u>·eh·ruhnt
– vegetarian	**– vegetariano ♂/vegetariana ♀** veh·zseh·tuh·ree·<u>uh</u>·noo ♂/ veh·zseh·tuh·ree·<u>uh</u>·nuh ♀
I'm allergic to…	**Sou alérgico ♂/alérgica ♀ a…** sauoo uh·<u>lehr</u>·gee·koo ♂/uh·<u>lehr</u>·gee·kuh ♀ uh…
I can't eat…	**Não posso comer…** nohm <u>paw</u>·soo koo·<u>mehr</u>…
– dairy	**– lacticínios** lahk·tee·<u>see</u>·nee·ooz
– gluten	**– glutina** gloo·<u>tee</u>·nuh
– nuts	**– nozes** <u>naw</u>·zehz
– pork	**– carne de porco** <u>kahrr</u>·neh deh <u>paur</u>·koo
– shellfish	**– molusco** moo·<u>loo</u>·skoo
– spicy foods	**– comidas pequantes** koo·<u>mee</u>·duhz pee·<u>kuhnts</u>
– wheat	**– trigo** <u>tree</u>·goo
– Is it *halal/kosher*?	**– É *halal/kosher*?** eh uh·<u>lahl</u>/<u>kaw</u>·shehr

Dining with Kids

Do you have children's portions?	**Tem porções das crianças?** teng poor·<u>soings</u> duhz kree·<u>uhn</u>·suhz
A child's seat, please.	**Um assento de criança, por favor.** oong uh·<u>sehn</u>·too deh kree·<u>uhn</u>·suh poor fuh·<u>vaur</u>
Where can I *feed/change* the baby?	**Onde posso *alimentar/mudar* o bebé [nenê]?** aund <u>paw</u>·soo uh·lee·mehn·<u>tahr</u>/moo·<u>dahr</u> oo beh·<u>beh</u> [neh·<u>neh</u>]
Can you warm this?	**Pode aquecer isto?** pawd uh·keh·<u>sehr</u> ee·stoo

▶ For travel with children, see page 155.

Complaints

How much longer will our food be?	**Quanto tempo demora a nossa comida?** <u>kwuhn</u>·too <u>tehm</u>·poo deh·<u>maw</u>·ruh uh <u>naw</u>·suh koo·<u>mee</u>·thuh
We can't wait any longer.	**Não podemos esperar mais.** nohm poo·<u>deh</u>·mooz ee·speh·<u>rahr</u> meyez
We're leaving.	**Vamo-nos embora.** <u>vuh</u>·moo·nooz ehm·<u>baw</u>·ruh
I didn't order this.	**Não encomendei isso.** nohm ehn·koo·mehn·<u>day</u> ee·soo
I ordered…	**Encomendei…** ehn·koo·mehn·<u>day</u>…
I can't eat this.	**Não posso comer isto.** nohm <u>paw</u>·soo koo·<u>mehr</u> ee·stoo
This is too…	**Isto está muito…** ee·stoo ee·<u>stah</u> <u>mooee</u>·too…
– cold/hot	**– fria/quente** <u>free</u>·uh/kehnt
– salty/spicy	**– salgado/picante** sahl·<u>gah</u>·thoo/pee·<u>kuhnt</u>
– tough/bland	**– árduo/insosso** <u>ahr</u>·dooau/een·<u>saw</u>·soo
This isn't *clean/fresh*.	**Isto não é *limpo/fresco*.** <u>ee</u>·stoo nohm eh <u>leem</u>·poo/<u>frehs</u>·koo

Paying

The check [bill], please.	**A conta, por favor.** uh <u>kaum</u>·tuh poor fuh·<u>vaur</u>
Separate checks [bills], please.	**Contas separadas, por favor.** <u>kaum</u>·tuhz seh·puh·<u>rah</u>·duhz poor fuh·<u>vaur</u>
It's all together.	**É tudo junto.** eh <u>too</u>·doo <u>zsoon</u>·too
Is service included?	**O serviço está incluído?** oo sehr·<u>vee</u>·soo ee·<u>stah</u> een·kloo·<u>ee</u>·thoo
What's this amount for?	**De que é esta quantitdade?** deh keh eh <u>eh</u>·stuh kwuhn·tee·<u>dahd</u>

I didn't have that. I had…	**Eu não tive aquele. Eu tive…** ehoo nohm teev uh·<u>kehl</u>. ehoo teev…
Can I pay by credit card?	**Posso pagar com cartão de crédito?** <u>paw</u>·soo puh·<u>gahr</u> kaum kuhr·<u>tohm</u> deh <u>kreh</u>·dee·too
Can I have *an itemized bill/a receipt*?	**Pode dar-me *uma conta detalhada/uma factura [um recibo]*?** pawd <u>dahr</u>·meh *<u>oo</u>·muh <u>kaum</u>·tuh deh·tuh·<u>lyah</u>·duh/<u>oo</u>·muh fah·<u>too</u>·ruh [oong reh·<u>see</u>·boo]*
That was a very good meal.	**Foi uma refeição excelente.** foy <u>oo</u>·muh reh·fay·<u>sohm</u> eh·seh·<u>lehnt</u>

Portuguese food is inspired by its location off the Atlantic Ocean; much of its cuisine consists of fish, especially salted cod. A lot of typical Portuguese food is the simple fare of fisherman and farmers. Expect to find fish, meat, rice and potatoes, combined with olive oil and wine. Restaurant owners and wait staff are generally extremely friendly.

Market

Where are the carts [trolleys]/baskets?	**Onde estão os carrinhos/cestos?** aund ee·<u>stohm</u> ooz kuh·<u>rree</u>·nyooz/<u>sehs</u>·tooz
Where is…?	**Onde é…?** aund eh…

▶ For food items, see page 89.

I'd like *some of that/those*.	**Queria *disso/desses*.** keh·<u>ree</u>·uh *<u>thee</u>·soo/<u>theh</u>·sehz*
Can I taste it?	**Posso provar?** <u>paw</u>·soo proo·<u>vahr</u>
I'd like…	**Queria…** keh·<u>ree</u>·uh…
– a *kilo/half-kilo* of…	**– um *quilo/meio quilo* de…** oong <u>kee</u>·loo/ <u>may</u>·oo <u>kee</u>·loo deh…
– a *liter/half-liter* of…	**– um *litro/meio litro* de…** oong <u>lee</u>·troo/ <u>may</u>·oo <u>lee</u>·troo deh…

I'd like…	**Queria…** keh·<u>ree</u>·uh…
– a piece of…	**– uma fatia de…** <u>oo</u>·muh fuh·<u>tee</u>·uh deh…
– a slice of…	**– um pedaço de…** oong peh·<u>dah</u>·soo deh…

▶For conversion tables, see page 184.

More/Less.	**Mais./Menos.** meyez/<u>meh</u>·nooz
How much?	**Quanto é?** <u>kwuhn</u>·too eh
Where do I pay?	**Onde pago?** aund <u>pah</u>·goo
A bag, please.	**Un saco, por favor.** oong <u>sah</u>·koo poor fuh·<u>vaur</u>
I'm being helped.	**Alguem está-me ajudar.** ahl·<u>geng</u> ee·<u>stah</u>·meh uh·zsoo·<u>dahr</u>

You May Hear…

Deseja alguma coisa? deh·<u>zeh</u>·zsuh ahl·<u>goo</u>·muh <u>coy</u>·zuh	Would you like something?
O que é que deseja? oo kee eh keh deh·<u>zeh</u>·zsuh	What would you like?
Mais alguma coisa? meyez ahl·<u>goo</u>·muh <u>coy</u>·zuh	Anything else?
São…euros. sohm…<u>ehoo</u>·rooz	That's…euros.

i Street markets are an integral part of Portuguese life, but you must get there early to get the full experience. By 10:00 a.m. the best things are gone. Most markets are held in the town square on a weekly basis. Everything can be found here—from the best foods, antiques and handicrafts to household items and clothes. Larger towns and cities may have covered markets that are open Monday through Saturday where you can buy fresh fish, meat, fruit and vegetables. Portuguese cheese, both delicious and inexpensive, is one of the most popular items at any market.

You May See...

USAR ATÉ...	best if used by...
CALORIAS	calories
SEM GORDURA	fat free
MANTER REFRIGERADO	keep refrigerated
PODE CONTER VESTÍGIOS DE...	may contain traces of...
DATA DE VENDA...	sell by...
PRÓPRIO PARA VEGETARIANOS	suitable for vegetarians

Dishes, Utensils and Kitchen Tools

bottle opener	**o abre-garrafas [abridor de garrafas]** oo ah·breh guh·rrah·fuhz [uh·bree·daur deh guh·rrah·fuhz]
bowl	**a malga** uh mahl·guh
can opener	**o abre-latas [abridor de latas]** oo ah·breh lah·tuhz [ah·bree·daur deh lah·tuhz]
corkscrew	**o saca-rolhas** oo sah·kuh rau·lyuhz
cups	**as chávenas [xícaras]** uhz shah·vee·nuhz [shee·kuh·ruhz]
forks	**os garfos** ooz gahr·fooz
frying pan	**a frigideira** uh free·zsee·thay·ruh
glasses	**os copos** ooz kaw·pooz
knife	**as facas** uhz fah·kuhz
measuring *cup/spoon*	**o copo/a colher** de medir oo kaw·poo/uh koo·lyehr deh meh·deer
paper napkin	**o guardanapo de papel** oo gwahr·duh·nah·poo deh puh·pehl

plates	**os pratos** ooz prah·tooz
pot	**a panela** uh puh·<u>neh</u>·luh
saucepan	**o tacho [a caçarola]** oo <u>tah</u>·shoo [uh kuh·suh·<u>rawl</u>·uh]
spatula	**a espátula** uh ees·<u>pah</u>·too·luh
spoon	**as colheres** uhz koo·<u>lyeh</u>·rehz

Meals

i **O pequeno almoço**
Breakfast (known **as café da manhã** in Brazil) is usually served from 7:00 to 10 a.m. In Portugal it consists of coffee, eggs, rolls, butter and jam. In Brazil, the addition of fresh fruit juice, fruit, toast and pastry makes for a heartier meal.

O almoço
Lunch is the main meal of the day, served from 12:30 to 2:30 p.m. Shops are normally closed during these hours. In Brazilian resorts, lunch is often served without interruption from 12:30 till evening. It generally consists of soup, fish or meat, and a dessert; salad might replace soup in Brazil.

O jantar
Dinner is served from about 7:30 to 9:30 p.m., except in a Portuguese **casa de fado** ("house of blues" dinner theater), where dinner is served a bit later. In Brazil dinner is from 8:00 to 11:00 p.m. Dinner typically consists of soup, fish or meat, salad, bread, and fruit for dessert. Coffee is almost always served at the end of every meal.

Breakfast

a agua uh <u>ah</u>·gwuh	water
o bolinho oo bau·lee·nyoo	muffin
o _café/chá_ oo kuh·<u>feh</u>/shah	coffee/tea
– com açúcar kaum uh·<u>soo</u>·kuhr	– with sugar
– com adoçante artificial kaum uh·thoo·<u>suhnt</u> uhr·tee·fee·see·<u>ahl</u>	– with artificial sweetner
– com leite kaum layt	– with milk
– descafeinado dehz·kuh·fay·<u>nah</u>·thoo	– decaf
– bica [cafezinho] <u>bee</u>·kuh [kuh·feh·<u>zee</u>·nyoo]	– black
as carnes frias uhz <u>kahr</u>·nehz <u>free</u>·uhz	cold cuts [charcuterie]
o cereal (_frio/quente_) oo seh·ree·<u>ahl</u> (<u>free</u>·oo/kehnt)	(_cold/hot_) cereal
o doce de fruta [geleia] oo <u>dau</u>·seh deh froo·tuh [zseh·<u>lay</u>·uh]	jam
a farinha de aveia uh fuh·<u>ree</u>·nyuh deh uh·<u>vay</u>·uh	oatmeal
o leite oo layt	milk
a manteiga uh muhn·tay·guh	butter
a omelete uh aw·meh·leh·tuh	omelet
o ovo... oo <u>au</u>·voo...	...egg
– muito fervido/fervido macio <u>mooee</u>·too fehr·<u>vee</u>·thoo/fehr·<u>vee</u>·thoo muh·<u>see</u>·oo	– hard-boiled/ soft-boiled
– estrelado [frito] ee·struh·<u>lah</u>·doo [<u>free</u>·too]	– fried
– mexido meh·<u>shee</u>·doo	– scrambled

I'd like...	**Queria...** keh·<u>ree</u>·uh...
More..., please.	**Mais..., se faz favor.** meyez...seh fahz fuh·<u>vaur</u>

o pão oo pohm	bread
o papo–seco [pãozinho] oo pah·poo seh·koo [pohm·zee·nyoo]	roll
o queijo oo kay·zsoo	cheese
as salsichas uhz sahl·see·shuhz	sausages
o sumo [suco] de... oo soo·moo [soo·koo] deh	...juice
– fruta froo·tuh	– fruit
– maça muh·suh	– apple
– toranja uh taw·ruhn·zsuh	– grapefruit
– laranja luh·ruhn·zsuh	– orange
o toicinho oo toy·see·nyoo	bacon
as torradas uhz too·rrah·duhz	toast
o yogurte oo yaw·goort	yogurt

Appetizers [Starters]

as carnes frias uhz kahr·nehz free·uhz	cold cuts
o chouriço oo shauoo·ree·soo	sausage
as lulas à milanesa uhz loo·luhz ah mee·luh·neh·zuh	squid
o paio oo peye·oo	smoked pork fillet (Port.)
os pimentos assados ooz pee·mehn·tooz uh·sah·dooz	roasted peppers
o pipis oo pee·peez	spicy chicken stew
a santola recheada uh suhn·taw·luh reh·shee·ah·thuh	stuffed crab

With/ Without...	Com/Sem... kaum/seng...
I can't have...	Não posso ter... nohm paw·soo tehr...

Soup

o caldo verde oo <u>kahl</u>·doo vehrd — potato and kale soup with sausage

o gaspacho oo guhz·<u>pah</u>·shoo — chilled soup with tomatoes, sweet peppers, onions, cucumbers and croutons

as migas de bacalhau uhz <u>mee</u>·guhz deh buh·kuh·<u>lyahoo</u> — dried cod soup with garlic and bread

a sopa açorda à Alentejana a <u>sau</u>·puh uh·<u>saur</u>·duh ah uh·luhn·teh·<u>zsuh</u>·nuh — bread soup with garlic and herbs

a sopa de cozido a <u>sau</u>·puh deh koo·<u>zee</u>·doo — meat broth with vegetables and macaroni

a sopa seca uh <u>sau</u>·puh <u>seh</u>·kuh — thick soup with meat, cabbage and bread

a sopa transmontana a <u>sau</u>·puh truhnz·moo·<u>tuh</u>·nuh — vegetable soup with bacon and bread

a sopa... uh <u>sau</u>·puh... — ...soup

– à pescador ah pehs·kuh·<u>daur</u> — – fish

– canja <u>keng</u>·zsuh — – chicken and rice

– de abóbora <u>deh</u> uh·<u>baw</u>·buh·ruh — – pumpkin

– de agriões deh uh·gree·<u>oings</u> — – potato and watercress

– de coentros deh koo·<u>eng</u>·trooz — – coriander, bread, and poached eggs

– de ervilhas deh eer·<u>vee</u>·lyuhz — – green pea

I'd like...	**Queria...** keh·<u>ree</u>·uh...
More..., please.	**Mais..., se faz favor.** meyez...seh fahz fuh·<u>vaur</u>

75

Fish and Seafood

o atum oo uh·<u>toong</u> — tuna

as amêijoas à bulhão pato uhz uh·<u>may</u>·zsoo·uhz ah boo·<u>lyohm</u> pah·too — clams with coriander, garlic and onion

as amêijoas à portuguesa uhz uh·<u>may</u>·zsoo·uhz ah poor·too·<u>geh</u>·zuh — clams with garlic, parsley and olive oil

o bacalhau à gomes de sá oo buh·kuh·<u>lyahoo</u> ah <u>gau</u>·mehz deh sah — dried cod with olives, garlic, onions, parsley and hard-boiled eggs

o bacalhau podre oo buh·kuh·<u>lyahoo</u> <u>pau</u>·dreh — baked layers of cod and fried potatoes

a cabeça de pescada cozida uh kuh·<u>beh</u>·suh deh peh·<u>skah</u>·thuh koo·<u>zee</u>·thuh — fish stew

os camarões... ooz kuh·muh·<u>roings</u>... — ...shrimp [king prawns]

– **fritos** <u>free</u>·tooz — fried

– **grandes** <u>gruhn</u>·dehz — large shrimp [king prawns] (Braz.)

– **no espeto** noo ee·<u>speh</u>·too — on a stick (Braz.)

a caldeirada... uh kahl·day·<u>rah</u>·thuh... — fish with onions, tomatoes, potatoes and olive oil...

– **à fragateira** ah fruh·guh·<u>tay</u>·ruh — fish, shellfish and mussels in a fish stock with tomatoes

– **à moda da Póvoa** ah <u>maw</u>·duh duh <u>praw</u>·voo·uh — hake, skate, sea-bass and eel simmered with tomatoes in olive oil

With/Without...	**Com/Sem...** kaum/seng...
I can't have...	**Não posso ter...** nohm <u>paw</u>·soo tehr...

o espadarte oo ees·puh·<u>dahrt</u>	swordfish
a lagosta uh luh·<u>gau</u>·stuh	lobster
a lampreia uh luhm·<u>pray</u>·uh	lamprey
o linguado oo leeng·<u>gwah</u>·thoo	sole
as lulas uhz <u>loo</u>·luhz	squid
as lulas recheadas uhz <u>loo</u>·luhz reh·shee·<u>ah</u>·duhz	stuffed squid
os mariscos ooz muh·<u>rees</u>·kooz	seafood
a moqueca de peixe uh moo·<u>keh</u>·kuh deh paysh	stew made of fish, shellfish or shrimp with coconut milk (Braz.)
as ostras do Algarve uhz <u>aw</u>·struhz thoo ahl·<u>gahrv</u>	oysters in butter and wine (Algarve)
o pargo oo <u>pahr</u>·goo	bream
o polvo oo <u>paul</u>·voo	octopus
o vatapá oo vuh·tuh·<u>pah</u>	fish and shrimp in a paste made of flour or breadcrumbs (Braz.)

Meat and Poultry

o arroz de frango oo uh·<u>rrauz</u> deh <u>fruhn</u>·goo	chicken with white wine, ham and rice
o bife [filete] oo beef [fee·<u>leh</u>·chee]	steak
o bife na frigideira oo beef nuh free·zsuh·<u>day</u>·ruh	steak fried in butter, white wine and garlic
o borrego [carneiro] oo boo·<u>rreh</u>·goo [kuhr·<u>nay</u>·roo]	lamb
a carne de porco uh kahrn deh <u>paur</u>·koo	pork

| I'd like… | Queria… keh·<u>ree</u>·uh… |
| More…, please. | Mais…, se faz favor. meyez…seh fahz fuh·<u>vaur</u> |

a carne de sol com feijão verde uh kahrn deh sol kaum fay·zsohm vehrd — sun-dried meat (*jerky*) with green beans (Braz.)

a carne de vaca uh kahrn deh vah·kuh — beef

o carneiro guisado [ensopado] oo kuhrr·nay·roo gee·zah·thoo [eng·soo·pah·do] — mutton with tomatoes, garlic and herbs

o coelho oo koo·eh·lyoo — rabbit

a costeleta uh koo·stuh·leh·tuh — cutlet

o cozido à portuguesa oo koo·zee·doo ah poor·too·geh·zuh — boiled beef, bacon, smoked sausage and vegetables

a feijoada uh fay·zsoo·ah·duh — Brazil's national dish: black beans cooked with bacon, salted pork, jerky, and sausage

o frango oo fruhn·goo — chicken

o frango na púcara oo fruhn·goo nuh poo·keh·ruh — chicken stewed in port and cognac, then fried with almonds

o medalhão oo meh·duh·lyohm — tenderloin steak

o perdiz à caçador oo pehr·deez uh kuh·suh·daur — partridge simmered with carrots, onions, white wine and herbs

o presunto oo preh·zoon·too — cured ham

as tripas à moda do Porto uhz tree·puhz ah maw·duh thoo paur·too — tripe cooked with pork, beans and chicken

a vitela uh vee·tehl·uh — veal

With/Without...	Com/Sem... kaum/sehn...
I can't have...	Não posso ter... nohm paw·soo tehr...

o xinxim de galinha oo sheeng·<u>sheeng</u> deh guh·<u>lee</u>·nyuh — chicken cooked in dried shrimp, peanuts and parsley (Braz.)

rare	**mal passado** ♂ **/passada** ♀ mahl puh·<u>sah</u>·thoo ♂/puh·<u>sah</u>·thuh ♀
medium	**meio passado** ♂ **/passada** ♀ <u>may</u>·oo puh·<u>sah</u>·thoo ♂/puh·<u>sah</u>·thuh ♀
well-done	**bem passado** ♂ **/passada** ♀ beng puh·<u>sah</u>·thoo ♂/puh·<u>sah</u>·thuh ♀

In Portugal, many dishes are served with both rice and potatoes. Almost every meal is served with a salad. Portugal is not a very vegetarian-friendly country, and vegetarians will have a difficult time finding meals in restaurants outside of Lisbon or the Algarve.

I'd like...	**Queria...** keh·<u>ree</u>·uh...
More..., please.	**Mais..., se faz favor.** meyez...seh fahz fuh·<u>vaur</u>

Vegetables

o acarajé oo uh·kuh·ruh·<u>zseh</u>	grated beans fried in palm oil , served with pepper sauce, onions and shrimp (Braz.)
a álface uh ahl·<u>fah</u>·seh	lettuce
as cebolas uhz seh·<u>bau</u>·luhz	onions
os cogumelos ooz koo·goo·<u>meh</u>·looz	mushrooms
as ervilhas uhz eer·<u>vee</u>·lyuhz	peas
as favas uhz <u>fah</u>·vuhz	broad beans
o feijão oo fay·<u>zsohm</u>	kidney beans
o feijão verde oo fay·<u>zsohm</u> vehrd	green beans
os pimentos ooz pee·<u>mehn</u>·tooz	peppers
o rutu à mineira oo rroo·<u>too</u> ah mee·<u>nay</u>·ruh	beans, cassava, flour, pork, cabbage, fried eggs and bacon (Braz.)

Spices and Staples

o açafrão oo uh·suh·<u>frohm</u>	saffron
o açúcar oo uh·<u>soo</u>·kuhr	sugar
as alcaparras uhz ahl·kuh·<u>pah</u>·rruhz	capers
as amêndoas uhz uh·<u>mehn</u>·doo·uhz	almonds
o arroz... oo uh·<u>rrauz</u>...	rice...
– de alhos deh <u>ah</u>·lyooz	– with garlic

With/Without...	**Com/Sem...** kaum/sehn...
I can't have...	**Não posso ter...** nohm <u>paw</u>·soo tehr...

– **de cozido** deh koo·<u>zee</u>·thoo	– cooked in meat stock
– **de feijão** de fay·<u>zsohm</u>	– with beans
as batatas… uhz buh·<u>tah</u>·tuhz…	potatoes…
– **cozidas** koo·<u>zee</u>·duhz	– boiled
– **cozidas com pele** koo·<u>zee</u>·duhz kohm pehl	– boiled in their skins
– **fritas** <u>free</u>·tuhz	– fries [chips]
– **de palha** deh <u>pah</u>·lyuh	– matchsticks
o puré de batatas oo poo·<u>reh</u> deh buh·<u>tah</u>·tuhz	mashed potatoes
a farinha uh fuh·<u>ree</u>·nyuh	flour
o manjericão oo muhn·zseh·ree·<u>kohm</u>	basil
a manteiga uh muhn·<u>tay</u>·guh	butter
as massas uhz <u>mah</u>·suhz	pasta
o pão oo pohm	bread
a pimenta uh pee·<u>mehn</u>·tuh	black pepper
o sal o sahl	salt
a salsa uh <u>sahl</u>·suh	parsley

Fruit

o abacate oo uh·buh·<u>kaht</u>	avocado
o abacaxi oo uh·buh·<u>kah</u>·shee	pineapple
os alperces ooz uhl·<u>pehr</u>·sehz	apricots
as ameixas uhz uh·<u>may</u>·shuhz	plums

I'd like…	**Queria…** keh·<u>ree</u>·uh…
More…, please.	**Mais…, se faz favor.** meyez…seh fahz fuh·<u>vaur</u>

Portuguese	Pronunciation	English
a **banana**	uh buh·_nuh_·nuh	banana
as **cerejas**	uhz seh·_ray_·zsuhz	cherries
o **coco**	oo _kaw_·koo	coconut
a **fruta**	uh _froo_·tuh	fruit
a **goiaba**	uh goy·_ah_·buh	guava
a **laranja**	uh luh·_ruhn_·zsuh	orange
a **lima**	uh _lee_·muh	lime
o **limão**	oo lee·_mohm_	lemon
a **maçã**	uh muh·_suh_	apple
o **mamão**	oo muh·_mohm_	papaya
a **manga**	uh _muhn_·guh	mango
a **mexerica**	uh meh·sheh·_ree_·kuh	tangerine
a **melancia**	uh muh·luhn·_see_·uh	watermelon
o **melão**	oo meh·_lohm_	melon
os **morangos**	ooz moo·_ruhn_·gooz	strawberries
a **pêra**	uh _peh_·ruh	pear
o **pêssego**	oo _peh_·suh·goo	peach
a **toranja**	uh taw·_ruhn_·zsa	grapefruit
as **uvas**	uhz _oo_·vuhz	grapes
o **mirtilo**	oo meer·_tee_·loo	blueberry
o **arando**	oo uh·_ruhn_·doo	cranberry
a **framboesa**	uh fruhm·_booeh_·zuh	raspberry
o **kiwi**	oo kee·_wee_	kiwi

English	Portuguese	Pronunciation
With/Without…	**Com/Sem…**	kaum/sehn…
I can't have…	**Não posso ter…**	nohm _paw_·soo tehr…

Cheese

o azeitão oo uh·zay·<u>tohm</u>	creamy cheese
a bola uh <u>bau</u>·luh	hard cow's milk cheese
o cabreiro oo kuh·<u>bray</u>·roo	goat's milk cheese
o castelo branco oo kuh·<u>steh</u>·loo <u>bruhn</u>·koo	creamy blue cheese
a évora uh <u>eh</u>·voo·ruh	creamy cheese
a ilha uh <u>ee</u>·lyuh	cow's milk cheese from the Azores Islands (Port.)
o queijo oo <u>kay</u>·zsoo	cheese
o queijo de Minas oo·<u>kay</u>·zsoo deh <u>mee</u>·nuhz	Brazilian cow's milk cheese
o requeijão oo reh·kay·<u>zsohm</u>	creamy Brazilian cheese
macio muh·<u>see</u>·oo	soft
duro <u>doo</u>·roo	hard
suave <u>swahv</u>	mild
forte oo fawrt	strong

Dessert

a arrufada de Coimbra uh uh·rroo·<u>fah</u>·duh deh <u>kooeem</u>·bruh	cinnamon dough cake
a babá-de-moça uh buh·<u>bah</u> deh <u>mau</u>·suh	dessert made of egg yolk, coconut milk and syrup (Braz.)
o bolo podre oo <u>bau</u>·loo <u>pau</u>·dreh	honey and cinnamon cake

I'd like…	**Queria…** keh·<u>ree</u>·uh…
More…, please.	**Mais…, se faz favor.** meyez…seh fahz fuh·<u>vaur</u>

as broas castelares uhz <u>brau</u>·uhz kuh·steh·<u>lah</u>·rehz	sweet-potato biscuits
a canjica uh <u>kuhn</u>·zsee·kuh	dessert made with sweet corn and milk (Braz.)
a goiabada uh goy·uh·<u>bah</u>·duh	thick paste made of guavas (Braz.)
o mousse de maracujá oo <u>moo</u>·seh deh muh·ruh·koo·<u>zsah</u>	passion fruit mousse (Braz.)
os ovos moles de Aveiro ooz <u>aw</u>·vooz mawlz deh ah·<u>vay</u>·roo	egg yolks cooked in syrup
o pastel de Tentúgal oo puhz·<u>tehl</u> deh tehn·<u>too</u>·gahl	pastry filled with egg yolks cooked in syrup
pudim flan poo·<u>deeng</u> fluhn	caramel custard
quindim keeng·<u>deeng</u>	coconut and egg yolk pudding (Braz.)

Drinks

Essential

The *wine list/drink menu*, please.	**A *carta dos vinhos/ementa de bebidas*, se faz favor.** uh <u>kahr</u>·tuh dooz <u>vee</u>·nyooz/ ee·<u>mehn</u>·tuh deh beh·<u>bee</u>·duhz seh fahz fuh·<u>vaur</u>
What do you recommend?	**O que é que me recomenda?** oo keh eh keh meh reh·koo·<u>mehn</u>·duh
I'd like a *bottle/glass* of *red/white* wine.	**Queria *uma garrafa/um copo* de vinho *tinto/branco*.** keh·<u>ree</u>·uh <u>oo</u>·muh guh·<u>rrah</u>·fuh/ oong <u>kaw</u>·poo deh <u>vee</u>·nyoo <u>teen</u>·too/<u>bruhn</u>·koo
The house wine, please.	**O vinho da casa, se faz favor.** oo <u>vee</u>·nyoo duh <u>kah</u>·zuh seh fahz fuh·<u>vaur</u>

Another *bottle/glass*, please.	**Outra garrafa/Outro copo, se faz favor.** <u>auoo</u>·truh guh·<u>rrah</u>·fuh/<u>auoo</u>·troo <u>kaw</u>·poo ser fahz fuh·<u>vaur</u>
I'd like a local beer.	**Gostaria uma cerveja local.** goo·stuh·<u>ree</u>·uh <u>oo</u>·muh sehr·<u>vay</u>·zsuh loo·<u>kahl</u>
Can I buy you a drink?	**Deixa comprar-le uma bebida?** <u>day</u>·shuh kaum·<u>prahr</u>·leh <u>oo</u>·muh beh·<u>bee</u>·thuh
Cheers!	**Viva!** <u>vee</u>·vuh
A *coffee/tea*, please.	**Um *café/chá*, se faz favor.** oong kuh·<u>feh</u>/ shah seh fahz fuh·<u>vaur</u>
Black.	**bica [cafezinho]** <u>bee</u>·kuh [kuh·feh·<u>zee</u>·nyoo]
With…	**com…** kaum…
– milk	**– leite** layt
– sugar	**– açúcar** uh·<u>soo</u>·kuhr
– artificial sweetener	**– adoçante** uh·doo·<u>suhnt</u>
…, please.	**…, se faz favor.** …seh fahz fuh·<u>vaur</u>
– A juice	**– Um sumo [suco]** oong <u>soo</u>·moo [<u>soo</u>·koo]
– A soda	**– Um refresco** oong reh·<u>freh</u>·skoo
– A *sparkling/still* water	**– Uma água *com/sem* gás** <u>oo</u>·muh <u>ah</u>·gwuh *kaum/sehm* gahz
Is the tap water safe to drink?	**A agua de casa é boa de beber?** uh <u>ah</u>·gwuh eh <u>baw</u>·uh deh beh·<u>behr</u>

Drinks

a água de coco uh <u>ah</u>·gwuh deh <u>kau</u>·koo (Braz.)	coconut juice
a água *com/sem* gás uh <u>ah</u>·gwuh *kaum/sehn* gahz	*carbonated/ noncarbonated* [still] water
o chá frio oo shah <u>free</u>·oo	iced tea

o café oo kuh·feh — coffee

o caldo de cana oo kahl·doo deh kuh·nuh — sugar-cane juice (Braz.)

o leite oo layt — milk

o leite de coco oo layt deh kau·koo — coconut milk

o sumo [suco] oo soo·moo [soo·koo] — juice

o refresco oo reh·freh·skoo — soda

---

i In both Portugal and Brazil, look for the bars advertising **sumos** (juices) with lots of fresh fruit on display. **Sumol®** is the oldest brand name of fruit juice and is found in almost every shop selling food. It is a lightly carbonated orange drink.

You May Hear...

Posso oferecer-lhe uma bebida? paw·soo aw·freh·sehr·lyeh oo·muh beh·bee·thuh — Can I get you a drink?

Com *leite/açúcar?* kaum *layt/uh·soo·kuhr* — With *milk/sugar?*

Água com ou sem gás? ah·gwuh kaum auoo seng gahz — Carbonated or noncarbonated [still] water?

Aperitifs, Cocktails and Liqueurs

de aguardente… de ah·gwahr·thent…	tequila spirit with…
– de figo deh fee·goo	– fig
– de medronho deh meh·draw·nyoo	– arbutus berry (*a small strawberry-like fruit*)
– á velha ah veh·lyuh	– brandy
a batida… uh buh·tee·duh…	cane spirit with fruit juice, sugar, ice and…(Braz.)
– de caju deh kuh·zsoo	– cashew nut
– de coco deh kau·koo	– coconut
– de maracujá deh muh·ruh·koo·zsah	– passion fruit
a caipirinha uh keye·pee·ree·nyuh	cane spirit, crushed lime, sugar and ice (Braz.)
a Cuba livre uh koo·buh lee·vreh	rum and Coke®
a genebra uh zseh·neh·bruh	gin
a ginjinha uh zseeng·zsee·nyuh	spirit distilled from morello cherries
o uísque oo wees·keh	whiskey
o vermute oo vehr·moot	vermouth
a tequila uh teh·kee·luh	tequila
o rum oo roong	rum
a vodca uh vaw·dee·kuh	vodka

Beer

a cerveja uh sehr·vay·zsuh	beer
a cerveja branca uh sehr·vay·zsuh bruhn·kuh	lager

a cerveja preta uh sehr·<u>vay</u>·zsuh <u>preh</u>·tuh   dark beer

o imperial [um chope] oo eem·<u>peh</u>·ree·ahl   draft [draught] beer
[oo <u>shaw</u>·pee]

> *i*   Beer is a popular drink in Portugal and Brazil. Try local
> brews, such as **Sagres** in Portugal and **Antártica** in Brazil.
> In Portugal, beer is often served with **tremoços** (salted lupini
> beans) or **amendoins** (peanuts).

Wine

o vinho... oo <u>vee</u>·nyoo...   ...wine

– **da *casa/mesa*** duh <u>kah</u>·zuh/<u>meh</u>·zuh   – house/table

– **(da) Madeira** (thuh) muh·<u>thay</u>·ruh   – (from) Madeira

– **(do) Porto** (thoo) <u>paur</u>·too   – Port

– **espumante** ee·spoo·<u>muhnt</u>   – sparkling

– **seco/doce** <u>seh</u>·koo/<u>dau</u>·seh   – dry/sweet

– **tinto/branco/rosé** <u>teen</u>·too/<u>bruhn</u>·koo/rau·<u>zeh</u>   – red/white/blush [rosé]

– **verde** vehrd   – dry white wine

> *i*   Brazilian wines are produced in the southern part of the
> country, which turns out some good reds and whites. Labels
> to look for include **Almadén** and **Forestier**.
>
> Excellent red and white aperitif and dessert wines come from the
> island of Madeira; **Sercial** is the driest, and **Verdelho** (medium-
> dry) can be drunk as an aperitif; **Boal** (or **Bual**) is smoky and
> less sweet than the rich dark-amber **Malvásia** (or Malsey),
> which is best served as a dessert wine at room temperature.
>
> Port, famous fortified wine from the upper Douro valley, east
> of Oporto, is classified by vintage and blend. The vintage
> ports, only made in exceptional years, are harvested and left

to ferment for at least two years before being bottled, and then stored for ten to twenty years. The blended ports are kept in barrels for a minimum of five years. There are two types: the younger ruby variety (**tinto aloirado**) is full-colored and full-bodied, while the tawny (**aloirado**) is less sweet, amber-colored and delicate.

Vinho verde, green wine, produced in northwest Portugal, is made from unripened grapes. It is faintly sparkling and acidic in taste, with a low alcohol content.

Menu Reader

o abacate oo uh·buh·<u>kaht</u>	avocado
o abacaxi oo uh·buh·<u>kah</u>·shee	pineapple
a abóbora uh uh·<u>baw</u>·boo·ruh	pumpkin
o açafrão oo uh·suh·<u>frohm</u>	saffron

o **acarajé** oo uh·kuh·ruh·<u>zseh</u>	fried beans
o **açúcar** oo uh·<u>soo</u>·kuhr	sugar
o **agrião** oo uh·gree·<u>ohm</u>	watercress
a **água** uh <u>ah</u>·gwuh	water
a **água de coco** uh <u>ah</u>·gwuh deh <u>kau</u>·koo	coconut juice
a **água mineral** uh <u>ah</u>·gwuh mee·neh·<u>ral</u>	mineral water
o **aipo** oo ah·<u>ee</u>·poo	celery
a **alcachofra** uh ahl·kuh·<u>shau</u>·fruh	artichoke
as **alcaparras** uhz ahl·kuh·<u>pah</u>·rruhz	capers
o **alecrim** oo uh·leh·<u>kreeng</u>	rosemary
a **aletria** uh uhl·eh·<u>tree</u>·uh	sweet noodle pudding
a **alface** uh ahl·<u>fah</u>·seh	lettuce
o **Algarvia** oo uhl·guhr·<u>vee</u>·uh	almond layer cake
o **alheira** oo ah·<u>lyay</u>·ruh	sausage
o **alho** oo <u>ah</u>·lyoo	garlic
o **alho porro** oo <u>ah</u>·lyoo <u>pau</u>·rroo	leek
o **almoço** oo ahl·<u>mau</u>·soo	lunch
as **almôndegas** uhz ahl·<u>mawn</u>·deh·guhz	fishballs or meatballs
o **alperce** oo uhl·<u>pehr</u>·seh	apricot
as **amêijoas** uhz uh·<u>may</u>·zsoo·uhz	baby clams
as **ameixas** uhz uh·<u>may</u>·shuhz	plums
as **ameixas secas** uhz uh·<u>may</u>·shuhz <u>seh</u>·kuhz	prunes
a **amêndoa** uh uh·<u>mehn</u>·doo·uh	almond
o **amendoin** oo uh·mehn·doo·<u>eeng</u>	peanut
a **amora** uh uh·<u>maw</u>·ruh	blackberry
o **ananás** oo uh·nuh·<u>nahz</u>	pineapple
a **anchova** uh uhn·<u>shau</u>·vuh	anchovy

o **aperitivo** oo uh·pehr·uh·<u>tee</u>·voo	aperitif
o **arenque** oo uh·<u>rehn</u>·keh	herring
o **arroz** oo uh·<u>rrauz</u>	rice
o **arroz doce** oo uh·<u>rrauz</u> <u>dau</u>·seh	rice pudding
o **assado** oo uh·<u>sah</u>·thoo	roast
o **atum** oo uh·<u>toong</u>	tuna
a **aveia** uh uh·<u>vay</u>·uh	oats
a **avelã** uh uh·veh·<u>luh</u>	hazelnut
as **aves** uhz <u>ahv</u>·ehz	poultry
a **azeda** uh uh·<u>zeh</u>·duh	sorrel
azedo uh·<u>zeh</u>·thoo	sour
o **azeite** oo uh·<u>zay</u>·teh	oil
a **azeitona** uh uh·zay·<u>tau</u>·nuh	olive
o **bacalhau** oo buh·kuh·<u>lyahoo</u>	cod
a **banana** uh buh·<u>nuh</u>·nuh	banana
a **batata** uh buh·<u>tah</u>·tuh	potato
a **batata doce** uh buh·<u>tah</u>·tuh <u>dau</u>·seh	sweet potato
as **batatas fritas** uhz buh·<u>tah</u>·tuhz <u>free</u>·tuhz	fries [chips]
o **batido** oo buh·<u>tee</u>·thoo	milk shake
a **baunilha** uh bahoo·<u>nee</u>·lyuh	vanilla
a **bebida** uh beh·<u>bee</u>·thuh	drink
o **berbigão** oo behr·bee·<u>gohm</u>	type of cockle
a **beringela** uh behr·eeng·<u>zseh</u>·luh	eggplant [aubergine]
o **besugo** oo beh·<u>soo</u>·goo	bream (fish)
a **beterraba** uh beh·teh·<u>rrah</u>·buh	beet [beetroot]
o **bife** oo beef	steak

o bife acebolado oo beef uh·seh·boo·<u>lah</u>·thoo	steak with onions (Braz.)
a bola de Berlim uh <u>bau</u>·luh deh behr·<u>leeng</u>	doughnut
a bolacha uh boo·<u>lah</u>·shuh	cookie [biscuit]
a bolacha de água e sal uh boo·<u>lah</u>·shuh deh <u>ah</u>·gwuh ee sahl	cracker
o bolo oo <u>bau</u>·loo	pastry
o borrego oo boo·<u>rreh</u>·goo	lamb
as broas castelares uhz <u>brau</u>·uhz kuhz·tuh·<u>lay</u>·rehz	sweet-potato cookies
as broas de mel uhz <u>brau</u>·uhz deh mehl	corn flour and honey cookies
os brócolos ooz <u>braw</u>·koo·looz	broccoli
os bunuelos ooz boo·noo·<u>eh</u>·looz	dough fritters (Braz.)
o cabrito oo kuh·<u>bree</u>·too	kid
a caça uh <u>kah</u>·suh	game
o cacau oo kuh·<u>kahoo</u>	cocoa
o cachorro quente oo kuh·<u>shau</u>·roo kehnt	hot dog
o café oo kuh·<u>feh</u>	coffee
o caju oo kah·<u>zsoo</u>	cashew nut (Braz.)
a caldeirada uh kahl·day·<u>rah</u>·duh	fish stew
o caldo oo <u>kahl</u>·doo	consommé
o caldo de cana oo <u>kahl</u>·doo deh <u>kuh</u>·nuh	sugar-cane juice
o caldo verde oo <u>kahl</u>·doo vehrd	potato and kale soup
os camarões ooz kuh·muh·<u>roings</u>	shrimp
o canapé oo kuh·nuh·<u>peh</u>	small open sandwich
a canela uh kuh·<u>neh</u>·luh	cinnamon
a canja uh <u>keng</u>·juh	chicken soup with rice
o capão oo cuh·<u>pohm</u>	capon

o caqui oo kuh·<u>kee</u>	persimmon (Braz.)
o caracol oo kuh·ruh·<u>kawl</u>	snail; spiral bun with currants
o caranguejo oo kuh·ruhn·<u>gay</u>·zsoo	crab
o carapau oo kuh·ruh·<u>pahoo</u>	mackerel
o caril oo kuh·<u>reel</u>	curry powder
a carne de porco uh <u>kahr</u>·neh deh <u>paur</u>·koo	pork
a carne de sol uh <u>kahr</u>·neh deh sawl	sun-dried meat, jerky
a carne de vaca uh <u>kahr</u>·neh deh <u>vah</u>·kuh	beef
a carne picada uh <u>kahr</u>·neh pee·<u>kah</u>·thuh	minced meat
o carneiro oo kuhrr·<u>nay</u>·roo	mutton
as carnes uhz <u>kahr</u>·nehz	meat
as carnes frias uhz <u>kahr</u>·nehz <u>free</u>·uhz	[charcuterie] cold cuts
o caruru oo kuh·<u>roo</u>·roo	minced herbs in oil and spices (Braz.)
caseiro oo kuh·<u>zay</u>·roo	homemade
a casquinha de siri uh kuhz·<u>kee</u>·nyuh deh <u>see</u>·ree	crab in its shell (Braz.)
a castanha uh kuhz·<u>tuh</u>·nyuh	chestnut
a castanha de caju uh kuhz·<u>tuh</u>·nyuh deh <u>kah</u>·zsoo	cashew nut
a (água de) Castelo uh (<u>ah</u>·gwuh deh) kuh·<u>steh</u>·loo	carbonated mineral water
a cavala uh kuh·<u>vuh</u>·luh	mackerel
a cebola uh seh·<u>bau</u>·luh	onion
a cenoura uh seh·<u>nau</u>·ruh	carrot
a cereja uh seh·<u>ray</u>·zsuh	cherry
o chá oo shah	tea
o chá com leite oo shah kaum layt	tea with milk

o **chá com limão** oo shah kaum lee·<u>mohm</u>	tea with lemon
o **chá de limão** oo shah deh lee·<u>mohm</u>	tea made from lemon peel infusion
o **chá maté** oo shah muh·<u>teh</u>	tea infused with maté-tree leaf
o **cherne** oo <u>shehr</u>·neh	black grouper
a **chicória** uh shee·<u>kaw</u>·ree·uh	chicory
o **chispe** oo <u>sheez</u>·peh	pig's foot [trotter]
o **chocolate quente** oo shoo·koo·<u>laht</u> kehnt	hot chocolate
os **chocos** ooz <u>shau</u>·kooz	cuttlefish
o **chouriço** oo shaw·<u>ree</u>·soo	smoked pork sausage
o **chuchu** oo <u>shoo</u>·shoo	type of rutabaga (Braz.)
o **churrasco** oo shoo·<u>rahz</u>·koo	charcoal-grilled meat
as **cocadas** uhz caw·<u>cah</u>·duhz	coconut macaroons (Braz.)
o **coco** oo <u>kau</u>·koo	coconut
a **codorna** uh koo·<u>dawrr</u>·nuh	quail (Braz.)
o **codorniz** oo koo·dawrr·<u>neez</u>	quail
o **coelho** oo koo·<u>eh</u>·lyoo	rabbit
o **coentro** oo koo·<u>ehn</u>·troo	coriander
o **cogumelo** oo koo·goo·<u>meh</u>·loo	button mushroom
o **colorau** oo koo·loo·<u>rahoo</u>	paprika
os **cominhos** ooz koo·<u>mee</u>·nyooz	cumin
a **compota** uh koom·<u>paw</u>·tuh	compote, stewed fruit
os **condimentos** ooz kaum·dee·<u>mehn</u>·tooz	seasonings
o **congro** oo <u>kaum</u>·groo	conger eel
o **conhaque** oo kaw·<u>nyahk</u>	cognac
a **conta** uh <u>kaum</u>·tuh	bill

o copo oo <u>kaw</u>·poo	glass
o coração oo koo·ruh·<u>sohm</u>	heart
o cordeiro oo koor·<u>day</u>·roo	lamb
a corvina uh kawr·<u>vee</u>·nuh	croaker (fish)
a costeleta uh koo·stuh·<u>leh</u>·tuh	cutlet
a couve uh <u>kaw</u>·veh	cabbage
a couve portuguesa uh <u>kaw</u>·veh poor·too·<u>geh</u>·zuh	kale
a couve roxa uh <u>kaw</u>·veh <u>rau</u>·shuh	red cabbage
a couve-de-bruxelas uh <u>kaw</u>·veh de broo·<u>sheh</u>·luhz	brussels sprouts
a couve-flor uh <u>kaw</u>·veh flaur	cauliflower
a coxinha de galinha uh kaw·<u>shee</u>·nyuh deh guh·<u>lee</u>·nyuh	pastry filled with chicken
os cravinhos ooz kruh·<u>vee</u>·nyooz	cloves
o creme oo krehm	cream
o creme de abacate oo krehm deh uh·buh·<u>kaht</u>	avocado with lime juice and sugar (Braz.)
o crème leite oo krehm layt	custard
o crepe oo krehp	pancake
a criação uh kree·uh·<u>sohm</u>	poultry
cru kroo	raw
os crustáceos ooz kroo·<u>stah</u>·see·ooz	shellfish
o damasco oo duh·<u>mahs</u>·koo	apricot (Braz.)
a dendê uh dehn·<u>deh</u>	palm oil
o doce de abóbora oo thaus deh uh·<u>baw</u>·boo·ruh	pumpkin dessert
o doce de fruta [a geleia] oo thaus deh <u>froo</u>·tuh [uh zseh·<u>lay</u>·uh]	jam

o doce de laranja oo thaus de luh·<u>ruhn</u>·zsuh	marmalade
o doce de ovos e amêndoa oo thaus deh <u>aw</u>·vooz ee uh·<u>mehn</u>·doo·uh	marzipan
o eiró oo ay·<u>raw</u>	eel
a empadinha uh eem·puh·<u>thee</u>·nyuh	filled pastry
o empadão de batata oo eem·puh·<u>dohm</u> deh buh·<u>tah</u>·tuh	shepherd's pie
a enguia uh eng·<u>gee</u>·uh	eel
o ensopado de cabrito oo eng·soo·<u>pah</u>·thoo deh keh·<u>bree</u>·too	kid stew
a entrada uh ehn·<u>trah</u>·thuh	appetizer [starter]
o entrecosto oo ehn·treh·<u>kaus</u>·too	sparerib
a erva-doce uh <u>ehr</u>·vuh thaus	aniseed
as ervilhas uhz eer·<u>vee</u>·lyuhz	peas
escalfado ee·skahl·<u>fah</u>·thoo	poached
o espadarte oo ee·spah·<u>dahr</u>·teh	swordfish
os espargos ooz ees·<u>pahr</u>·gooz	asparagus
o espaguete oo ee·spuh·<u>geht</u>	spaghetti
os espinafres ooz ee·spee·<u>nah</u>·frehz	spinach
estufado ee·stoo·<u>fah</u>·thoo	braised
o esturjão oo ee·stoor·<u>zsohm</u>	sturgeon
a faisão uh feye·<u>zohm</u>	pheasant
a farinha uh fuh·<u>ree</u>·nyuh	flour
o farofel oo fuh·rau·<u>fehl</u>	cassava flour
as favas uhz <u>fah</u>·vuhz	broad beans
o feijão oo fay·<u>zsohm</u>	bean
o feijão branco oo fay·<u>zsohm</u> bruhn·koo	navy bean
o feijão catarino oo fay·<u>zsohm</u> kuh·tuh·<u>ree</u>·noo	pink bean

o feijão encarnado oo fay-<u>zsohm</u> eng-kuhrr-<u>nah</u>-thoo — red bean

o feijão frade oo fay-<u>zsohm</u> frahd — black-eyed bean

o feijão guisado [ensopado] oo fay-<u>zsohm</u> gee-<u>sah</u>-thoo [een-soo-<u>pah</u>-doo] — beans with bacon in tomato sauce

o feijão preto oo fay-<u>zsohm</u> preh-too — black bean

o feijão tropeiro oo fay-<u>zsohm</u> trau-<u>pay</u>-roo — black beans fried with jerky (Braz.)

o feijão verde oo fay-<u>zsohm</u> vehrd — green beans

o fiambre oo fee-<u>uhm</u>-breh — boiled ham

o fígado oo <u>fee</u>-guh-doo — liver

o figo oo <u>fee</u>-goo — fig

o filete oo fee-<u>leht</u> — fillet of fish

as filhós uhz fee-<u>lyawz</u> — fritters

o filé oo fee-<u>leh</u> — steak (Braz.)

o folhado oo foo-<u>lyah</u>-thoo — sweet puff-pastry

a framboesa uh fruhm-boo-<u>eh</u>-zuh — raspberry

o frango oo <u>fruhn</u>-goo — chicken

o frango assado oo <u>fruhn</u>-goo uh-<u>sah</u>-thoo — roast chicken

a fritada de peixe uh free-<u>tah</u>-duh deh paysh — deep-fried fish

a fruta uh <u>froo</u>-tuh — fruit

a fruta do conde uh <u>froo</u>-tuh thoo <u>kaum</u>-deh — custard apple

a fruta em calda uh <u>froo</u>-tuh eng <u>kahl</u>-duh — fruit in syrup

os frutos do mar ooz <u>froo</u>-tuhz thoo mahr — seafood

a fubá uh foo-<u>bah</u> — corn flour (Braz.)

a galantina uh guh-luhn-<u>tee</u>-nuh — pressed meat in gelatin

a galinha uh guh-<u>lee</u>-nyuh — stewing chicken

a galinhola uh guh-lee-<u>nyaw</u>-luh — woodcock

o **galão** oo guh·<u>lohm</u>	weak milky coffee
as **gambas** uhz <u>guhm</u>·buhz	shrimp [king prawns]
o **ganso** oo <u>guhn</u>·soo	goose
a **garoupa** uh guh·<u>rauoo</u>·puh	large grouper (fish)
a **garrafa** uh guh·<u>rrah</u>·fuh	bottle
a **gasosa** uh guh·<u>zaw</u>·zuh	lemonade
o **gaspacho** oo guhz·<u>pah</u>·shoo	chilled soup
o **gelado** oo zseh·<u>lah</u>·thoo	ice cream
a **gelatina** uh zseh·luh·<u>tee</u>·nuh	jelly
a **geleia** uh zseh·<u>lay</u>·uh	jelly (Braz.)
o **gelo** oo <u>zseh</u>·loo	ice
a **gengibre** uh zsehn·<u>zsee</u>·breh	ginger
a **goiaba** uh zsoy·<u>ah</u>·buh	guava (Braz.)
a **goiabada** uh zsoy·uh·<u>bah</u>·duh	thick paste made of guava (Braz.)
o **gombo** oo <u>gaum</u>·boo	okra (Braz.)
os **grelos** ooz <u>greh</u>·looz	turnip sprouts
a **groselha** uh groo·<u>zeh</u>·lyuh	red currant
o **guisado** oo gee·<u>zah</u>·thoo	stew
a **hortaliça** uh awr·tuh·<u>lee</u>·suh	fresh vegetables
a **hortelã** uh awr·teh·<u>luh</u>	mint
o **inhame** oo ee·<u>nuhm</u>	yam
oo **iogurte** oo yaw·<u>goort</u>	yogurt
a **isca de peixe** uh <u>ees</u>·kuh deh <u>paysh</u>	fried small fish (Braz.)
as **iscas** uhz <u>ees</u>·kuhz	sliced liver
o **jabuticaba** oo juh·boo·tee·<u>cah</u>·buh	type of cherry (Braz.)
a **jardineira** uh zsuhr·dee·<u>nay</u>·ruh	mixed vegetables
o **javali** oo zsuh·<u>vah</u>·li	wild boar

o kibe oo keeb	meat and bulgur croquette (Braz.)
a lagosta uh lah·gau·stuh	lobster
o lagostim oo luh·gau·steeng	crayfish
lagostim do-rio luh·gau·steeng doo ree·oo	fresh-water crayfish
a lampreia uh luhm·pray·uh	lamprey
a laranja uh luh·ruhn·zsuh	orange
a laranjada uh luh·ruhn·zsah·thuh	orange soda
o lavagante oo luh·vu·guhnt	lobster
o lebre oo leh·breh	hare
os legumes ooz leh·goomz	vegetables
o leite oo layt	milk
o leite de coco oo layt deh kau·koo	coconut milk
o leitão oo lay·tohm	suckling pig
as lentilhas uhz lehn·tee·lyuhz	lentils
o lima oo lee·muh	lime
o limão oo lee·mohm	lemon
oo limão verde oo lee·mohm vehrd	lime (Braz.)
a língua uh leen·gwuh	tongue
o linguado oo leen·gwah·doo	sole
a linguíça uh leen·gwee·suh	thin sausage
o lombo oo laum·boo	loin
o louro oo lau·roo	bay leaf
a lula uh loo·luh	squid
a maçã uh muh·suh	apple
o maçapão oo muh·suh·pohm	marzipan
o macarrão oo muh·kuh·rrohm	macaroni
a macaxeira uh muh·kuh·shay·ruh	cassava root (Braz.)

maduro muh·<u>thoo</u>·roo	ripe
a maionese uh meye·aw·<u>nehz</u>	mayonnaise
a malagueta uh muh·luh·<u>geh</u>·tuh	hot pepper
as malsadas uhz mahl·<u>sah</u>·duhz	fried dough (Braz.)
o mamão oo muh·<u>mohm</u>	papaya
a mandioca uh muhn·dee·<u>aw</u>·kuh	cassava root (Braz.)
a manga uh <u>muhn</u>·guh	mango
o manjericão oo muhn·zsehr·ee·<u>kohm</u>	basil
a manteiga uh muhn·<u>tay</u>·guh	butter
o maracujá oo muh·ruh·koo·<u>zsah</u>	passion fruit (Braz.)
os mariscos ooz muh·<u>rees</u>·kooz	seafood
a marmelada uh muhr·meh·<u>lah</u>·duh	thick quince paste
a massa uh <u>mah</u>·suh	pasta; dough; pastry
o massapão oo muh·suh·<u>pohm</u>	marzipan
os massapães ooz muh·suh·<u>pengz</u>	almond macaroons
o mate oo maht	tea with maté leaf (Braz.)
o medalhão oo meh·deh·<u>lyohm</u>	tenderloin steak
o medronho oo meh·<u>drau</u>·nyoo	arbutus berry (small strawberry-like fruit)
o mel oo mehl	honey
a melancia uh muh·luhn·<u>see</u>·uh	watermelon
o melão oo meh·<u>lohm</u>	melon
o melão com presunto oo meh·<u>lohm</u> kaum preh·<u>zoon</u>·too	melon with ham
o mero oo <u>meh</u>·roo	red grouper (*fish*)
a mexerica uh meh·sheh·<u>ree</u>·kuh	tangerine (Braz.)
os mexilhões ooz meh·shee·<u>lyoings</u>	mussels

as migas de bacalhau uhz <u>mee</u>·guhz deh buh·kuh·<u>lyahoo</u>	dried cod soup
o milho oo mee·<u>lyoo</u>	sweet corn
os miolos ooz mee·<u>aw</u>·looz	brains
o misto quente oo <u>mee</u>·stoo kehnt	ham-and-cheese toasted sandwich (Braz.)
o morango oo moo·<u>ruhn</u>·goo	strawberry
a morcela uh moor·<u>seh</u>·luh	blood sausage [black pudding]
a mortadela uh moor·tuh·<u>deh</u>·luh	mortadella
a mostarda uh moo·<u>stahr</u>·duh	mustard
o mousse de chocolate oo <u>moo</u>·seh deh shoo·koo·<u>laht</u>	chocolate pudding
o mousse de maracujá oo <u>moo</u>·seh deh muh·ruh·koo·<u>zsah</u>	passion fruit mousse
as nabiças uhz nuh·<u>bee</u>·suhz	turnip greens
os nabos ooz <u>nah</u>·booz	turnips
a nata uh <u>nah</u>·tuh	fresh cream
a nata batida uh <u>nah</u>·tuh buh·<u>tee</u>·duh	whipped cream
(ao) natural (ahoo) nuh·too·<u>rahl</u>	plain
as nêsperas uhz <u>neh</u>·speh·ruhz	loquat (fruit)
no forno noo <u>faurr</u>·noo	baked
a noz uh nawz	nut
a noz moscada uh nawz moo·<u>skah</u>·thuh	nutmeg
o óleo oo <u>aw</u>·lee·oo	oil
o óleo de amendoim oo <u>aw</u>·lee·oo deh uh·mehn·doo·<u>eeng</u>	peanut oil
a omelete uh aw·meh·<u>leht</u>	omelet
o orégão [orégano] oo aw·reh·<u>gohm</u>	oregano

o osso oo <u>au</u>·soo	bone
a ostra uh <u>aw</u>·struh	oyster
o ovo oo <u>aw</u>·voo	egg
os ovos cozidos ooz <u>aw</u>·vooz koo·<u>zee</u>·thooz	boiled eggs
os ovos escalfados ooz <u>aw</u>·vooz ees·kahl·<u>fah</u>·thooz	poached eggs
os ovos estrelados [fritos] ooz <u>aw</u>·vooz ees·truh·<u>lah</u>·dooz [<u>free</u>·tooz]	fried eggs
os ovos mexidos ooz <u>aw</u>·vooz meh·<u>shee</u>·dooz	scrambled eggs
os ovos quentes ooz <u>aw</u>·vooz kehntz	soft-boiled eggs
o palmito oo pahl·<u>mee</u>·too	palm hearts (Braz.)
panado [empanado] puh·<u>nah</u>·thoo [ehm·puh·<u>nah</u>·doo]	breaded
a panqueca uh puhn·<u>keh</u>·kuh	pancake
o pão (escuro/integral) oo pohm (ees·<u>koo</u>·roo/een·teh·<u>grahl</u>)	bread (brown/whole wheat)
o pão de centeio oo pohm deh sehn·<u>tay</u>·oo	rye bread
o pão-de-ló oo pohm·deh·<u>law</u>	coffee cake
o pãozinho oo pohm·<u>zee</u>·nyoo	bread roll
o pargo oo <u>pahr</u>·goo	bream (*fish*)
passado puh·<u>sah</u>·thoo	cooked (*meat, etc.*)
a passa (de uva) uh <u>pah</u>·suh (deh <u>oo</u>·vuh)	raisin
o pastel oo puhs·<u>tehl</u>	small pie
o pato oo <u>pah</u>·too	duck
o pé de moleque oo peh deh maw·<u>leh</u>·keh	peanut brittle (Braz.)
o peito de galinha oo <u>pay</u>·too deh guh·<u>lee</u>·nyuh	chicken breast
o peixe oo paysh	fish

o **peixe-agulh** oo paysh·uh·<u>gool</u> — garfish

o **peixe-espada** oo paysh ees·<u>pah</u>·duh — swordfish

o **pepino** oo peh·<u>pee</u>·noo — cucumber

o **pepino de conserva** oo peh·<u>pee</u>·noo deh kaum·<u>sehr</u>·vuh — pickle [gherkin]

a **pêra** uh <u>peh</u>·ruh — pear

a **perca** uh <u>pehr</u>·kuh — perch

o **perdiz** oo pehr·<u>deez</u> — partridge

a **perna de galinha** uh <u>pehrr</u>·nuh deh guh·<u>lee</u>·nyuh — chicken leg

o **pernil** oo perr·<u>neel</u> — ham

o **pêro** oo <u>peh</u>·rau — variety of apple

o **peru** oo peh·<u>roo</u> — turkey

os **pés de porco** ooz pehz deh <u>paur</u>·koo — pig's feet [trotters]

a **pescada** uh pehz·<u>kah</u>·thuh — whiting

o **pêssego** oo <u>peh</u>·suh·goo — peach

os **petiscos** ooz peh·<u>tees</u>·kooz — appetizers [starters]

a **pevide** uh peh·<u>veed</u> — salted pumpkin seed

a **picanha desfiada** uh pee·<u>kuh</u>·nyuh dehs·fee·<u>ah</u>·thuh — charcoal-grilled meat (Braz.)

os **pikles** ooz <u>pee</u>·kehlz — pickled vegetables

a **pimenta** uh pee·<u>mehn</u>·tuh — pepper

os **pimentos assados** ooz pee·<u>mehn</u>·tooz uh·<u>sah</u>·dooz — roasted peppers

a **pinhoada** uh pee·nyoo·<u>ah</u>·duh — pine nut brittle

o **pinhão** oo pee·<u>nyohm</u> — nut

o **pipis** oo pee·<u>peez</u> — spicy giblet stew

o **pirarucu** oo pee·ruh·<u>roo</u>·koo — type of fish (Braz.)

o **piri-piri** oo <u>pee</u>·ree <u>pee</u>·ree	seasoning of hot chili pepper and olive oil
o **polvo** oo <u>paul</u>·voo	octopus
o **pombo** oo <u>paum</u>·boo	pigeon
o **porco** oo <u>paur</u>·koo	pork
a **posta** uh <u>paws</u>·tuh	slice of fish or meat
o **presunto** oo preh·<u>zoon</u>·too	cured ham
o **presunto cru** oo preh·<u>zoon</u>·too kroo	dried ham
o **pudim flan** oo poo·<u>deeng</u> fluhn	caramel custard
o **puré de batatas** oo poo·<u>reh</u> deh buh·<u>tah</u>·tuhz	mashed potatoes
a **queijada** uh kay·<u>zsah</u>·duh	small cottage-cheese tart
o **queijinhos do céu** oo kay·<u>zsee</u>·nyooz doo sehoo	marzipan balls rolled in sugar
o **queijo** oo <u>kay</u>·zsoo	cheese
o **quiabo** oo kee·<u>ah</u>·boo	okra
o **quindim** oo <u>keeng</u>·deeng	pudding made with coconut and egg yolks (Braz.)
a **rabanada** uh ruh·buh·<u>nah</u>·duh	French toast
o **rabanete** oo ruh·buh·<u>neht</u>	radish
a **raia** uh <u>reye</u>·uh	skate (fish)
a **rainha-cláudia** uh ray·<u>ee</u>·nyuh <u>klaw</u>·dee·uh	greengage plum
recheado reh·shee·<u>ah</u>·thoo	stuffed
o **recheio** oo re·<u>shay</u>·oo	stuffing
o **refogado** oo reh·foo·<u>gah</u>·thoo	onions fried in olive oil
o **refresco** oo reh·<u>frehs</u>·koo	soft drink
o **repolho** oo rreh·<u>pau</u>·lyoo	cabbage

o requeijão oo rre·kay·<u>zsohm</u>	curd cheese (Braz.)
o rin oo rreeng	kidney
o robalo oo <u>rraw</u>·buh·loo	sea bass
o rodízio oo rroo·<u>dee</u>·zee·oo	selection of chargrilled meats (Braz.)
a romã uh rraü·<u>muh</u>	pomegranate
a rosca uh <u>rraus</u>·kuh	ring-shaped white bread
o rosmaninho oo rrooz·muh·<u>neeng</u>·nyoo	rosemary
o ruivo oo rroo·<u>ee</u>·voo	red gurnard (fish)
o sal oo sahl	salt
a salada uh suh·<u>lah</u>·duh	salad
a salada de *alface/ escarola* uh suh·<u>lah</u>·duh deh *ahl·<u>fah</u>·sehl/ees·kuh·<u>raw</u>·luh*	green salad
a salada de agrião uh suh·<u>lah</u>·duh deh uh·gree·<u>ohm</u>	watercress salad
a salada mista uh suh·<u>lah</u>·duh <u>mees</u>·tuh	tomato and lettuce salad
salgado sahl·<u>gah</u>·thoo	salted
o salmonete oo sahl·moo·<u>neht</u>	red mullet
o salmão (fumado) [defumado] oo suh·<u>mohm</u> (foo·<u>mah</u>·thoo)[deh·foo·<u>mah</u>·do]	(smoked) salmon
a salsa uh <u>sahl</u>·suh	parsley
a salsicha uh sahl·<u>see</u>·shuh	sausage
salteado sahl·tee·<u>ah</u>·thoo	sautéed
a salva uh <u>sahl</u>·vuh	sage
as sandes uhz suhndz	sandwich
a sanduíche uh suhn·doo·<u>eesh</u>	sandwich
a santola uh suhn·<u>taw</u>·luh	spider-crab

o sarapatel oo suh·ruh·puh·<u>tehl</u>	pork or mutton stew
a sarda uh <u>sahr</u>·thuh	mackerel
as sardinhas uhz suhr·<u>dee</u>·nyuhz	sardines
o sável oo <u>sah</u>·vehl	shad (herring-like fish)
seco <u>seh</u>·koo	dry
a sêmola uh <u>seh</u>·moo·luh	semolina
a sericá alentejano uh seh·ree·<u>kah</u> uh·lehn·teh·<u>zsuh</u>·noo	cinnamon soufflé
a sidra uh <u>see</u>·druh	cider
o siri oo <u>see</u>·ree	crab (Braz.)
as sobremesas uhz <u>sau</u>·breh·<u>meh</u>·zuhz	dessert
a solha uh <u>sau</u>·lyuh	plaice (fish)
o sonho oo <u>sau</u>·nyoo	type of doughnut
a sopa uh <u>sau</u>·puh	soup
o sorvete oo sawr·<u>veht</u>	ice cream (Braz.)
o sumo [suco] oo <u>soo</u>·moo [<u>soo</u>·koo]	fruit juice
o sururu oo soo·<u>roo</u>·roo	type of cockle (Braz.)
o suspiro oo soo·<u>spee</u>·roo	meringue
a taínha uh tah·<u>ee</u>·nyuh	gray mullet (fish)
a tâmara uh <u>tuh</u>·muh·ruh	date
a tangerina uh tuhn·zsuh·<u>ree</u>·nuh	tangerine
o tarte de amêndoa oo tahrt de uh·<u>mehn</u>·doo·uh	almond tart
o tempero oo <u>tehm</u>·peh·roo	seasoning
tenro <u>tehn</u>·rroo	tender
o tomate oo too·<u>maht</u>	tomato
o tomilho oo too·<u>mee</u>·lyoo	thyme
a toranja uh tau·<u>ruhn</u>·zsuh	grapefruit

as torradas uhz too·<u>rrah</u>·duhz	toast
o torrão de ovos oo too·<u>rrohm</u> deh <u>aw</u>·vooz	marzipan candy
a tosta uh <u>taw</u>·stuh	toasted sandwich
o toucinho oo tau·<u>see</u>·nyoo	bacon
o tremoço oo treh·<u>maw</u>·soo	salted lupin bean
a trufa uh <u>troo</u>·fuh	truffle
a truta uh <u>troo</u>·tuh	trout
o tucupi oo too·<u>koo</u>·pee	cassava juice (Braz.)
o tutano oo <u>too</u>·tuh·noo	marrow
o umbu oo <u>oom</u>·boo	tropical fruit (Braz.)
as uvas uhz <u>oo</u>·vuhz	grapes
as vagens uhz <u>vah</u>·gehnz	green beans
variado vuh·ree·<u>ah</u>·thoo	assorted
o veado oo vee·<u>ah</u>·thoo	venison
os vegetais variados ooz veh·zseh·<u>teyez</u> vuh·ree·<u>ah</u>·thooz	mixed vegetables
o vieira oo vee·<u>ay</u>·ruh	scallop
o vinagre oo vee·<u>nah</u>·greh	vinegar
a vitela uh vee·<u>tehl</u>·uh	veal

▼ *People*

Essential

Hello.	**Olá.** aw·lah
How are you?	**Como está?** kau·moo ee·stah
Fine, thanks.	**Bem, obrigado** ♂/**obrigada** ♀. behm aw·bree·gah·doo ♂/aw·bree·gah·duh ♀
Excuse me! (*to get attention*)	**Desculpe!** dehz·kool·peh
Do you speak English?	**Fala inglês?** fah·luh eeng·lehz
What's your name?	**Como se chama?** kau·moo seh shuh·muh
My name is…	**Chamo-me… [Meu nome é…]** shuh·moo meh… [mehoo naum·ee eh…]
Nice to meet you.	**Muito prazer.** mooee·too pruh·zehr
Where are you from?	**De onde é?** deh aund eh
I'm from the *U.S./U.K.*	**Sou *dos Estados Unidos/da Inglaterra.*** soh *dooz ee·stah·dooz oo·nee·dooz/ duh eeng·luh·teh·rruh*
What do you do?	**O que é que faz?** oo kee eh keh fahz
I work for…	**Trabalho para…** truh·bah·lyoo puh·ruh…
I'm a student.	**Sou estudante.** sauoo ee·stoo·duhnt
I'm retired.	**Sou reformado** ♂/**reformada** ♀. **[aposentado** ♂/**aposentada** ♀]** soh reh·foor·mah·thoo ♂/reh·foor·mah·thuh ♀ [uh·poo·zehn·tah·doo ♂/uh·poo·zehn·tah·duh ♀]
Do you like…?	**Gosta de…?** gaw·stuh deh…
Goodbye.	**Adeus.** uh·deeooz
See you later.	**Até mais tarde.** uh·teh meyez tahrd

Communication Difficulties

Do you speak English?	**Fala inglês?** <u>fah</u>·luh eeng·<u>lehz</u>
Does anyone here speak English?	**Há aqui alguém que fale inglês?** ah uh·<u>kee</u> ahl·<u>gehng</u> keh <u>fah</u>·leh eeng·<u>lehz</u>
I don't speak (much) Portuguese.	**Não falo (muito) português.** nohm <u>fah</u>·loo (<u>mooee</u>·too) poor·too·<u>gehz</u>
Could you speak more slowly?	**Pode falar mais devagar?** pawd fuh·<u>lahr</u> meyez deh·vuh·<u>gahr</u>
Could you repeat that?	**Pode repetir?** pawd reh·peh·<u>teer</u>
Excuse me? [Pardon?]	**Faça favor?** <u>fah</u>·suh fuh·<u>vaur</u>
What was that?	**Como disse?** <u>kau</u>·moo <u>dee</u>·seh
Could you spell it?	**Pode soletrar?** pawd sau·leh·<u>trahr</u>
Please write it down.	**Escreva, por favor.** ee·<u>screhv</u> poor fuh·<u>vaur</u>
Can you translate this for me?	**Pode traduzir-me isto?** pawd truh·doo·<u>zeer</u>·meh <u>ee</u>·stoo
What does *this/that* mean?	**O que significa *isto/aquilo*?** oo keh sehg·nee·<u>fee</u>·kuh <u>ee</u>·stoo/uh·<u>kee</u>·loo
I understand.	**Compreendo [Entendo].** kaum·pree·<u>ehn</u>·doo [ehn·<u>tehn</u>·doo]
I don't understand.	**Não compreendo [entendo].** nohm kaum·pree·<u>ehn</u>·doo [ehn·<u>tehn</u>·doo]
Do you understand?	**Entende?** ehn·<u>tehn</u>·deh

You May Hear...

Falo só um poco de Inglês. fah·loo saw oong pau·koo deh eeng·lehz
I only speak a little English.

Nao falo Inglês. nohm fah·loo eeng·lehz
I don't speak English.

Making Friends

Hello.	**Olá.** aw·lah
Good morning.	**Bom dia.** bong dee·uh
Good afternoon.	**Boa tarde.** baw·uh tahrd
Good evening.	**Boa noite.** baw·uh noyt
My name is...	**Chamo-me... [Meu nome é...]** shuh·moo meh... [mehoo naum·ee eh...]
What's your name?	**Como se chama?** kau·moo seh shuh·muh
I'd like to introduce you to...	**Gostaria de te introduzir á...** goo·stuh·ree·uh deh the een·troo·doo·zeer ah...
Nice to meet you.	**Muito prazer.** mooee·too preh·zehr
How are you?	**Como está?** kau·moo ee·stah
Fine, thanks.	**Bem, obrigado ♂/obrigada ♀.** beng aw·bree·gah·doo ♂/aw·bree·gah·duh ♀
And you?	**E o senhor ♂/a senhora ♀?** ee oo seh·nyaur ♂/uh seh·nyau·ruh ♀

In both Portugal and Brazil, a standard greeting is a handshake accompanied by direct eye contact and the appropriate greeting for the time of day. Once a closer relationship has developed, greetings become more personal: men may greet each other with a hug, and women kiss each other twice on the cheek starting with the right. Anyone with

a university degree is referred to as **Senhor Doutour** (literally, "Mr. Doctor") if male or **Senhora Doutoura** (Ms. Doctor) if female. Wait until invited before moving to a first-name basis.

Travel Talk

I'm here…	**Estou aqui…** ee·<u>staw</u>oo uh·<u>kee</u>…
– on business	**– em negócios** eng neh·<u>gaw</u>·see·yooz
– on vacation [holiday]	**– de férias** deh <u>feh</u>·ree·uhz
– studying	**– a estudar [estudando]** uh ee·stoo·<u>dahr</u> [ee·stoo·<u>duhn</u>·doo]
I'm staying for…	**Fico por…** <u>fee</u>·koo poor…
I've been here…	**Eu já estive aqui…** ehoo zsah ee·<u>stee</u>·veh uh·<u>kee</u>…
– a day	**– um dia** oong <u>dee</u>·uh
– a week	**– uma semana** <u>oo</u>·muh seh·<u>muh</u>·nuh
– a month	**– um mês** oong mehz

▶For numbers, see page 177.

Where are you from?	**De onde é?** deh aund eh
I'm from…	**Sou…** sawoo…

Relationships

Who are you with?	**Com quem está?** kaun keng ee·<u>stah</u>
I'm on my own.	**Estou sozinho** ♂/**sozinha** ♀. ee·<u>stawoo</u> saw·<u>zee</u>·nyoo ♂/saw·<u>zee</u>·nyuh ♀
I'm with my…	**Estou com *o meu* ♂/*a minha* ♀…** ee·<u>stawoo</u> kaum *oo mehoo* ♂/*uh <u>mee</u>·nyuh* ♀…
– husband/wife	– **marido/mulher** muh·<u>ree</u>·thoo/moo·<u>lyehr</u>
– boyfriend/girlfriend	– **namorado/namorada** nuh·moo·<u>rah</u>·thoo/ nuh·moo·<u>rah</u>·thuh
– friend(s)	– **amigo(s)** ♂/**amiga(s)** ♀ uh·<u>mee</u>·goo(z) ♂/ uh·<u>mee</u>·guh(z) ♀
– colleague(s)	– **colega(s)** koo·<u>leh</u>·guh(z)
When's your birthday?	**Quando fazes anos?** <u>kwuhn</u>·doo <u>fah</u>·zehz <u>uh</u>·noos
How old are you?	**Quantos anos tems?** <u>kwuhn</u>·tooz <u>uh</u>·noos tengz
I'm…	**Eu tenho…** ehoo <u>teh</u>·nyoo…

▶For numbers, see page 177.

Are you married?	**É casado** ♂/**casada** ♀**?** eh kuh·<u>zah</u>·doo ♂/ kuh·<u>zah</u>·duh ♀
I'm…	**Sou…/Estou…** sawoo/ee·<u>stawoo</u>…
– single	– **solteiro** ♂/**solteira** ♀ saul·<u>tay</u>·roo ♂/ (saul·<u>tay</u>·ruh) ♀
– in a relationship	– **num relacionamento** noong reh·luh·see·oo·nuh·<u>mehn</u>·too

I'm...	**Sou.../Estou...** sawoo/ee·<u>staw</u>oo...
– married	– **casado** ♂/**casada** ♀ kuh·<u>zah</u>·doo ♂/kuh·<u>zah</u>·duh ♀
– divorced	– **divorciado** ♂/**divorciada** ♀ dee·voor·see·<u>ah</u>·doo ♂/dee·voor·see·<u>ah</u>·duh ♀
– separated	– **separado** ♂/**separada** ♀ seh·puh·<u>rah</u>·doo ♂/seh·puh·<u>rah</u>·duh ♀
I'm widowed.	**Sou viuvo** ♂/**viuva** ♀. sau vee·<u>oo</u>·voo ♂/vee·<u>oo</u>·vuh ♀
Do you have *children/grandchildren*?	**Tem *filhos/netos*?** teng *fee·lyooz/neh·tooz*

Work and School

What do you do?	**O que é que faz?** oo kee eh keh fahz
What are you studying?	**O que é que está a estudar [estudando]?** oo kee eh keh ee·<u>stah</u> uh ee·stoo·<u>dahr</u> [ee·stoo·<u>duhn</u>·doo]
I'm studying...	**Estudo...** ee·<u>stoo</u>·doo...
I work *full time/part time*.	**Trabalho *tempo integral/meio tempo*.** truh·<u>bah</u>·lyoo *tehm·poo een·teh·grahl/may·oo tehm·poo*
I'm between jobs.	**Estou entre empregos.** ee·<u>staw</u>oo <u>ehn</u>·treh ehng·<u>preh</u>·gooz
I work at home.	**Trabalho de casa.** truh·<u>bah</u>·lyoo deh <u>kah</u>·zuh
Who do you work for?	**Para quem trabalha?** <u>puh</u>·ruh keng truh·<u>bah</u>·lyuh
I work for...	**Trabalho para...** truh·<u>bah</u>·lyoo <u>puh</u>·ruh...
Here's my business card.	**Aqui está meu cartão.** uh·<u>kee</u> ee·<u>stah</u> mehoo kuhr·<u>tohm</u>

▶ For business travel, see page 152.

Weather

What's the weather forecast?	**Quais são as previsões do tempo?** kweyez sohm uhz preh·vee·_zoings_ thoo tehm·poo
What _beautiful/terrible_ weather!	**Que tempo tão _lindo/ruin_!** keh _tehm_·poo tohm _leen·dool/rroo·eeng_
It's _cool/warm._	**Está _fresco/calor._** ee·_stah_ _frehs·kool/kuh·laur_
It's _rainy/sunny._	**Está um dia de _chuva/sol._** ee·_stah_ oong dee·uh deh _shoo·vuh/sawl_
It's _snowy/icy._	**Está um dia _de neve/com gelo._** ee·_stah_ oong dee·uh deh nehv/kaum _zseh·loo_
Do I need _a jacket/an umbrella_?	**Preciso de um _casaco/ sombreiro_?** preh·_see_·zoo deh oong kuh·_zah_·koo/saum·_bray_·roo

▶For temperature, see page 184.

Romance

Essential

Would you like to go out for _a drink/ dinner_?	**Queres ir _fóra tomar uma bebida/comer fóra_?** keh·rehz eer _faw·ruh too·mahr oo·muh_ beh·_bee_·thuh/_koo_·mehr _faw_·ruh
What are your plans for _tonight/tomorrow_?	**Quais são os seus planos para _hoje à noite/amanhã_?** kweyez sohm ooz sehooz pluh·nooz puh·ruh auzseh ah noyt/uh·muh·_nyuh_
Can I have your number?	**Pode dar-me o seu número de telefone?** pawd _dahr_·meh oo sehoo _noo_·meh·roo deh tehl·_fawn_
Can I join you?	**Posso acompanhar-te?** _paw_·soo uh·kaum·puh·_nyahr_·teh

Can I buy you a drink?	**O que quer beber?** oo keh kehr beh·<u>behr</u>
I like you.	**Gosto de ti.** <u>gawzh</u>·too deh tee
I love you.	**Te amo.** teh <u>uh</u>·moo

Making Plans

Would you like to go out for…?	**Queres ir fóra para…?** kehrz eer <u>faw</u>·ruh <u>puh</u>·ruh…
– coffee	**– um café** oong kuh·<u>feh</u>
– a drink	**– uma bebida** <u>oo</u>·muh beh·<u>bee</u>·thuh
– dinner	**– jantar** zsuhn·<u>tahr</u>
What are your plans for…?	**Quais são os seus planos para…?** kweyez sohm ooz sehooz <u>pluh</u>·nooz <u>puh</u>·ruh…
– tonight	**– hoje à noite** auzseh ah noyt
– tomorrow	**– amanhã** uh·muh·<u>nyuh</u>
– this weekend	**– este fim de semana** ehst feeng deh seh·<u>muh</u>·nuh
Where would you like to go?	**Onde queres ir?** aund kehrz eer
I'd like to go to…	**Quero ir à…** <u>keh</u>·roo eer ah…
Do you like…?	**Gosta de…?** <u>gaw</u>·stuh deh…
Can I have your *number/e–mail*?	**Pode dar-me o seu *número de telefone/ e-mail*?** pawd <u>dahr</u>·meh oo sehoo *<u>noo</u>·meh·roo deh tehl·<u>fawn</u> / ee·<u>mehl</u>*

▶ For e-mail and phone, see page 52.

Pick-Up [Chat-Up] Lines

Can I join you?	**Posso acompanhar-te?** paw·soo uh·kaum·puh·<u>nyahr</u>·teh
You look great!	**Está linda!** ee·<u>stah</u> <u>leen</u>·duh
Let's go somewhere quieter.	**Vamos para um sítio [lugar] mais sossegado.** <u>vuh</u>·mooz puh·ruh oong <u>see</u>·tyoo [loo·<u>gahr</u>] meyez soo·seh·<u>gah</u>·thoo

Accepting and Rejecting

I'd love to.	**Adorava [adoraria] ir.** uh·daw·<u>rah</u>·vuh [uh·doo·ruh·<u>ree</u>·uh] eer
Where should we meet?	**Onde nos vamos encontrar?** aund nooz <u>vuh</u>·mooz ehng·kaun·<u>trahr</u>
I'll meet you at *the bar/your hotel.*	**Vou ter consigo [te encontrar] ao** *bar/hotel.* vauoo tehr kaun·<u>see</u>·goo [tee ehn·kaun·<u>trahr</u>] ahoo *bahr/<u>aw</u>·tehl*
I'll come by at…	**Eu passo por la ás…** ehoo <u>pah</u>·soo poor lah ahz…

What's your address?	**Qual é a sua morada [endereço]?** kwahl eh uh soo·uh maw·rah·duh [ehn·deh·reh·soo]
I'm busy.	**Mas tenho imenso [muito] que fazer.** muhz teh·nyoo ee·mehn·soo [mooee·too] keh fuh·zehr
I'm not interested.	**Não estou interesado ♂/interesada ♀.** nohm ee·stawoo een·treh·sah·thoo ♂/ een·treh·sah·thuh ♀
Leave me alone.	**Deixe-me em paz.** day·sheh· meh eng pahz
Stop bothering me!	**Está quiéto!** ee·stah kee·eh·too

Getting Physical

Can I *hug/kiss* you?	**Posso te dar um *abraço/beijo*?** paw·soo teh dahr oong uh·brah·soo/bay·zsoo
Yes.	**Sim.** seeng
No.	**Não.** nohm
Stop!	**Para!** pah·ruh

Sexual Preferences

Are you gay?	**Ès homosexual?** ehz aw·maw·sehk·soo·ahl
I'm...	**Sou...** sauoo...
– heterosexual	**– heterossexual** eh·teh·raw·sehk·soo·ahl
– homosexual	**– homosexual** aw·maw·sehk·soo·ahl
– bisexual	**– bissexual** bee·sehk·soo·ahl
Do you like *men/ women*?	**Gosta de *homens/mulheres*?** gaw·stuh deh aw·mengz/moo·lyehrz

▶ For informal and formal "you," see page 173.

▼ Fun

Sightseeing

Essential

Where's the tourist office?	**Onde é o posto de turismo [informações turísticas]?** aund eh oo <u>pau</u>·stoo deh too·<u>reez</u>·moo [een·foor·muh·<u>soings</u> too·<u>ree</u>·stee·kuhz]
What are the main points of interest?	**O que há de mais interessante para se ver?** oo kee ah deh meyez een·tehr·reh·<u>suhnt</u> puh·ruh seh vehr
Do you have tours in English?	**Tem excursões em inglês?** teng ee·skoor·<u>soings</u> eng eng·<u>lehz</u>
Can I have a *map/ guide*?	**Pode dar-me um *mapa/guia*?** pawd <u>dahr</u>·meh oong *<u>mah</u>·puh/ <u>gee</u>·uh*

Tourist Information Office

Do you have any information on...?	**Tem qualquer informação sobre...?** teng kwahl·<u>kehr</u> een·foor·muh·<u>sohm</u> sau·breh...
Can you recommend...?	**Pode recomendar-me...?** pawd reh·koo·mehn·<u>dahr</u>·meh...
– a boat trip	**– uma excursão de barco** <u>oo</u>·muh ee·skoor·<u>sohm</u> deh <u>bahr</u>·koo
– an excursion	**– uma excursão** <u>oo</u>·muh ee·skoor·<u>sohm</u>
– a sightseeing tour	**– um circuito turístico** oong seer·koo·<u>ee</u>·too too·<u>ree</u>·stee·koo

In Brazil and Portugal, town maps and brochures on main tourist attractions are available at airports and from tourist information centers. Ask at your hotel or check online to find the nearest office.

Tours

I'd like to go on the tour to…	**Gostaria ir na excursão para…** goo·stuh·<u>ree</u>·uh eer nuh ee·skoor·<u>sohm</u> puh·ruh…
When's the next tour?	**Quando é a próxima excursão?** <u>kwuhn</u>·doo eh uh <u>praw</u>·see·muh ee·skoor·<u>sohm</u>
Are there tours in English?	**Há excursões em inglês?** ah ee·skoor·<u>soings</u> eng eeng·<u>lehz</u>
Is there an English-speaking *guide/audio guide*?	**Há *algum guia que fale inglês/uma gravação da visita guiada em inglês*?** ah ahl·<u>goong</u> <u>gee</u>·uh keh <u>fah</u>·leh eeng·<u>lehz</u>/<u>oo</u>·muh gruh·vuh·<u>sohm</u> deh vee·<u>zee</u>·tuh gee·<u>ah</u>·duh eng eeng·<u>lehz</u>
What time *do we leave/return*?	**Quando *saímos/regressemos*?** <u>kwuhn</u>·doo suh·<u>eemooz</u>/reh·<u>greh</u>·seh·mooz
We'd like to see…	**Gostaríamos de ver…** goo·stuh·<u>ree</u>·uh·mooz deh vehr…
Can we stop here…?	**Podemos parar aqui…?** poo·<u>deh</u>·mooz puh·<u>rahr</u> uh·<u>kee</u>…
– to take photographs	**– para tirar fotografias** <u>puh</u>·ruh tee·<u>rahr</u> foo·too·gruh·<u>fee</u>·uhz
– to buy souvenirs	**– para comprar lembranças** <u>puh</u>·ruh kaum·<u>prahr</u> leng·<u>bruhn</u>·suhz
– to use the restrooms [toilets]	**– para usar as casas de banho [os banheiros]** <u>puh</u>·ruh oo·<u>zahr</u> uhz <u>kah</u>·zuhz deh <u>buh</u>·nyoo [ooz buh·<u>nyay</u>·rooz]
Is there access for the disabled?	**Há algum acesso para os deficientes?** ah ahl·<u>goong</u> uh·<u>seh</u>·soo puh·ruh ooz deh·fee·see·<u>ehntz</u>

▶ For ticketing, see page 21.

▶ For the disabled, see page 158.

Sights

Where *is/are*...?	**Onde *é/são*...?** aund *eh/sohm*...
– the battleground	– **o campo de batalha** oo <u>kuhm</u>·poo deh buh·<u>tah</u>·lyuh
– the botanical garden	– **o jardim botânico** oo zsuhr·<u>deeng</u> boo·<u>tuh</u>·nee·koo
– the castle	– **o castelo** oo kuhz·<u>teh</u>·loo
– the downtown area	– **o centro da cidade** oo <u>sehn</u>·troo duh see·<u>dahd</u>
– the fountain	– **a fonte** uh <u>faun</u>·teh
– the library	– **a biblioteca** uh bee·blee·aw·<u>teh</u>·kuh
– the market	– **o mercado** oo mehr·<u>kah</u>·doo
– the museum	– **o museu** oo moo·<u>zehoo</u>
– the old town	– **a parte velha da cidade** uh pahrt <u>veh</u>·lyuh duh see·<u>dahd</u>
– the palace	– **o palácio** oo puh·<u>lah</u>·see·yoo
– the park	– **o parque** oo <u>pahr</u>·keh
– the ruins	– **as ruínas** uhz roo·<u>een</u>·uhz
– the shopping area	– **a zona comercial** uh <u>zau</u>·nuh koo·mehr·see·<u>ahl</u>
– the town square	– **o centro do povo** oo <u>sehn</u>·troo thoo <u>pau</u>·voo
Can you show me on the map?	**Pode indicar-me no mapa?** pawd een·dee·<u>kahr</u>·meh noo <u>mah</u>·puh

▶ For directions, see page 36.

Impressions

It's...	**É...** eh...
– amazing	– **espantoso** ee·spuhn·<u>tau</u>·zoo
– beautiful	– **lindo** <u>leen</u>·doo

– boring	– **aborrecido** uh·boo·rreh·<u>see</u>·thoo
– interesting	– **interessante** een·teh·reh·<u>suhnt</u>
– magnificent	– **magnífico** mahg·<u>nee</u>·fee·koo
– romantic	– **romântico** roo·<u>muhn</u>·tee·koo
– strange	– **estranho** ee·<u>struh</u>·nyoo
– stunning	– **estupendo** ee·stoo·<u>pehn</u>·doo
– terrible	– **horrível** aw·<u>rree</u>·vehl
– ugly	– **feio** <u>fay</u>·oo
I (don't) like all of it.	**(Não) gosto de tudo.** (nohm) <u>gaw</u>·stoo deh <u>too</u>·thoo

Religion

Where's…?	**Onde é…?** aund eh…
– the cathedral	– **a catedral** uh keh·teh·<u>drahl</u>
– the *Catholic/ Protestant* church	– **a igreja *católica/protestante*** uh ee·<u>gray</u>·zsuh kuh·<u>taw</u>·lee·kuh/praw·tee·<u>stuhnt</u>
– the mosque	– **a mesquita** uh mehz·<u>kee</u>·tuh

123

Where's...?	**Onde é...?** aund eh...
– the shrine	**– o relicário** oo reh·lee·<u>kah</u>·ree·oo
– the synagogue	**– a sinagoga** uh seen·uh·<u>gaw</u>·guh
– the temple	**– o templo** oo <u>tehm</u>·ploo
What time is *mass/ the service*?	**A que horas é *a missa/o culto*?** uh kee <u>aw</u>·ruhz eh *uh <u>mee</u>·suh/oo <u>kool</u>·too*

Shopping

Essential

Where is the *market/ mall [shopping center]*?	**Onde é *o mercado/a zona comercial*?** aund eh *oo mehr·<u>kah</u>·thoo/uh <u>zau</u>·nuh koo·mehr·see·<u>ahl</u>*
I'm just looking.	**Estou só a ver [vendo].** ee·<u>stawoo</u> saw uh vehr [<u>vehn</u>·doo]
Can you help me?	**Pode ajudar-me?** pawd uh·zsoo·<u>dahr</u>·meh
I'm being helped.	**Alguem está-me ajudar.** ahl·<u>gehng</u> ee·<u>stah</u>·meh uh·zsoo·<u>dahr</u>
How much is it?	**Quanto é?** <u>kwuhn</u>·too eh
That one, please.	**Aquele, por favor.** uh·<u>kehl</u> poor fuh·<u>vaur</u>
That's all, thanks.	**É tudo, obrigado ♂/obrigada ♀.** eh <u>too</u>·doo aw·bree·<u>gah</u>·doo ♂/aw·bree·<u>gah</u>·thuh ♀
Where can I pay?	**A onde pago?** uh aund <u>pah</u>·goo
I'll pay *in cash/by credit card*.	**Pago *a dinheiro/com o cartão de crédito*.** <u>pah</u>·goo *uh dee·<u>nyay</u>·roo/kaun oo kuhr·<u>tohm</u> deh <u>kreh</u>·dee·too*
A receipt, please.	**Um recibo, se faz favor.** oong reh·<u>see</u>·boo seh fahz fuh·<u>vaur</u>

Flea markets in Portugal are common in almost every town and usually occur once a week or every other week (in smaller towns). These are the best places to get the most for your money. Haggling is common and almost expected. It is rare to pay full price for anything except food, for which prices are generally not negotiable. Bring cash, as few vendors accept credit cards.

Stores

Where *is/are*...?	**Onde *é/são*...?** aund *eh/sohm*...
– the antiques store	– **a loja das antigüidades** uh <u>law</u>·zsuh duhz uhn·tee·gee·<u>dah</u>·dehz
– the bakery	– **a padaria** uh pah·deh·<u>ree</u>·uh
– the bank	– **o banco** oo <u>buhn</u>·koo
– the bookstore	– **a livraria** uh lee·vreh·<u>ree</u>·uh
– the clothing store	– **a loja de artigos de vestuário** uh <u>law</u>·zsuh deh uhr·<u>tee</u>·gooz de veh·stoo·<u>ah</u>·ree·oo
– the delicatessen	– **a charcutaria** uh shuhr·koo·tuh·<u>ree</u>·uh
– the department store	– **o grande armazém [a loja de departamentos]** oo gruhnd uhr·muh·<u>zeng</u> [uh <u>law</u>·zsuh deh deh·puhr·tuh·<u>mehn</u>·tooz]
– the gift shop	– **a loja de recordações** uh <u>law</u>·zsuh deh reh·kaur·duh·<u>soingz</u>
– the health food store	– **a loja de produtos dietéticos** uh <u>law</u>·zsuh deh proo·<u>doo</u>·tooz dee·<u>eh</u>·tee·kooz
– the jeweler	– **a joalharia [joalheria]** uh zsoo·uh·lyuh·<u>ree</u>·uh [zsoo·uh·lyeh·<u>ree</u>·uh]
– the liquor store [off-licence]	– **a loja de vinhos** uh <u>law</u>·zsuh deh <u>vee</u>·nyooz
– the market	– **o mercado** oo mehr·<u>kah</u>·doo

Where *is*/*are*...?	**Onde** *él**são*...? aund *eh*/*sohm*...
– the pastry shop	– **a pastelaria [confeitaria]** uh puh·stuh·luh·<u>ree</u>·uh [kaun·fay·tuh·<u>ree</u>·uh]
– the pharmacy [chemist]	– **a farmácia** uh fuhr·<u>mah</u>·see·uh
– the produce [grocery] store	– **a frutaria [quitanda]** uh froo·tuh·<u>ree</u>·uh [kee·<u>tuhn</u>·duh]
– the shoe store	– **a sapataria** uh suh·puh·tuh·<u>ree</u>·uh
– the shopping mall [shopping centre]	– **a zona comercial** uh <u>zau</u>·nuh koo·mehr·see·<u>ahl</u>
– the souvenir store	– **a loja de lembranças** uh <u>law</u>·zsuh deh lehn·<u>bruhn</u>·suhz
– the supermarket	– **o supermercado** oo soo·pehr·mehr·<u>kah</u>·thoo
– the tobacconist	– **a tabacaria** uh tuh·bah·kuh·<u>ree</u>·uh
– the toy store	– **o armazém [a loja] de brinquedos** oo ahr·muh·<u>zehn</u> [uh <u>law</u>·zsuh] deh breeng·<u>keh</u>·dooz

Services

Can you recommend…?	**Pode recomendar-me…?** pawd reh·koo·mehn·<u>dahr</u>·meh…
– a barber	**– o cabeleireiro de homens** oo kuh·beh·lay·<u>ray</u>·roo deh <u>aw</u>·mengs
– a dry cleaner	**– a lavandaria de limpeza a seco** uh luh·vuhn·duh·<u>ree</u>·uh deh leeng·<u>peh</u>·zuh uh <u>seh</u>·koo
– a hairdresser	**– o cabeleireiro de senhoras** oo kuh·beh·lay·<u>ray</u>·roo deh see·<u>nyau</u>·ruhz
– a laundromat [launderette]	**– a lavandaria [lavanderia]** uh luh·vuhn·duh·<u>ree</u>·uh [uh luh·vuhn·deh·<u>ree</u>·uh]
– a nail salon	**– o salão das unhas** oo suh·<u>lohm</u> duhz <u>oo</u>·nyuhz
– a spa	**– a estância de saúde** uh ee·<u>stuhn</u>·see·uh deh suh·<u>ooth</u>
– a travel agency	**– a agência de viagens** uh ah·<u>zsehn</u>·see·uh deh vee·<u>ah</u>·zsengs
Can you…this?	**Pode…isto?** pawd…<u>ee</u>·stoo
– alter	**– modificar** moo·dee·fee·<u>kahr</u>
– clean	**– limpar** leem·<u>parh</u>
– mend	**– consertar** kaun·sehr·<u>tahr</u>
– press	**– engomar** eeng·goo·<u>mahr</u>
When will it be ready?	**Quando estará pronto?** <u>kwuhn</u>·doo ee·stuh·<u>rah</u> <u>praun</u>·too

Spa

I'd like…	**Queria…** keh·<u>ree</u>·uh…
– *an eyebrow/a bikini wax*	**– uma cera de *sobrancelha/biquíni*** <u>oo</u>·muh <u>seh</u>·ruh deh *sau·bruhn·<u>seh</u>·lyuhz/ bee·<u>kee</u>·nee*

I'd like...	**Queria...** keh·<u>ree</u>·uh...
– a facial	– **uma limpeza de pele** <u>oo</u>·muh leem·<u>peh</u>·zuh deh <u>pehl</u>
– a *manicure/ pedicure*	– **uma manicure/um pedicuro** <u>oo</u>·muh muh·nee·<u>koor</u>/oong peh·dee·<u>koo</u>·roo
– a (sports) massage	– **uma massagem (d'esportes)** <u>oo</u>·muh mehn·<u>sah</u>·zseng (dee·<u>spawr</u>·tehz)
Do you do...?	**Faz...?** fahz...
– acupuncture	– **acupuntura** uh·koo·poon·<u>too</u>·ruh
– aromatherapy	– **aromaterapia** uh·raw·muh·teh·reh·<u>pee</u>·uh
– oxygen treatment	– **tratamento de oxigênio** truh·tuh·<u>mehn</u>·too deh awk·see·<u>zseh</u>·nee·oo
Is there a sauna?	**Há sauna?** ah <u>sahoo</u>·nuh

---

i

Portugal, well-known for the benefits of its natural mineral waters, is filled with healing and wellness centers that cater to people with all sorts of illnesses. Contact the **Associaçao das Termas de Portugal** (Association of Facilities of Portugal) for a list of centers throughout Portugal.

In Portugal and Brazil, check with your hotel concierge for information on local spas that offer massage, acupuncture and skin treatments. These spa centers are most often found in large cities. Tipping is usually included in the price, but an additional 10% tip is appreciated for extraordinary service.

Hair salon

I'd like...	**Queria...** keh·<u>ree</u>·uh...
– an appointment for *today/tomorrow*	– **fazer uma marcação [marcar um horário] para *hoje/amanhã*** fuh·<u>zehr</u> <u>oo</u>·muh mahr·kuh·<u>sohm</u> [muhr·<u>kahr</u> oong aw·<u>rah</u>·ree·oo] puh·ruh *auzseh/uh·muh·<u>nyuh</u>*
– some color	– **alguma cor** ahl·<u>goo</u>·muh kaur

– some highlights	– **madeixas** muh·<u>day</u>·shuhz
– my hair styled	– **meu cabelo penteado** mehoo kuh·<u>beh</u>·loo pehn·tee·<u>ah</u>·thoo
– a haircut	– **um corte** oong kawrt
– a trim	– **acertar as pontas [aparar]** uh·sehr·<u>tahr</u> uhz <u>paun</u>·tuhz [uh·puh·<u>rahr</u>]
Don't cut it too short.	**Não corte muito curto.** nohm kawrt <u>mooee</u>·too <u>koor</u>·too
Shorter here.	**Mais curto aqui.** meyez <u>koor</u>·too uh·<u>kee</u>

Sales Help

What are the opening hours?	**O que são as horas de abertura?** oo keh sohm uhz <u>aw</u>·ruhz deh ah·behr·<u>too</u>·ruh
Where *is/are*...?	**Onde *él são*...?** aund *eh/sohm*...
– the cashier	– **a caixa** uh <u>keye</u>·shuh
– the escalator	– **a escada rolante** uh ees·<u>kah</u>·duh roo·<u>luhnt</u>
– the elevator [lift]	– **o elevador** oo eh·leh·vuh·<u>daur</u>
– the fitting room	– **os vestuários** ooz vehs·too·<u>ah</u>·ree·ooz
– the store directory [guide]	– **a planta da loja** uh <u>pluhn</u>·tuh duh <u>law</u>·zsuh
Can you help me?	**Pode ajudar-me?** pawd uh·zsoo·<u>dahr</u>·meh
I'm just looking.	**Estou só a ver [vendo].** ee·<u>stawoo</u> saw uh vehr [<u>vehn</u>·doo]
I'm being helped.	**Alguem está-me ajudar.** ahl·<u>geng</u> ee·<u>stah</u>·meh uh·zsoo·<u>dahr</u>
Do you have...?	**Tem...?** teng...
Could you show me...?	**Podia mostrar-me...?** poo·<u>dee</u>·uh mooz·<u>trahr</u>·meh...

Can you *ship it / wrap it*?	**Pode *despachá-lo / embrulhá-lo*?** pawd *dehs-puh-shah-loo/eng-broo-lyah-loo*
How much is it?	**Quanto é?** kwuhn-too eh
That's all, thanks.	**É tudo, obrigado ♂ /obrigada ♀.** eh too-doo aw-bree-gah-doo ♂ /aw-bree-gah-duh ♀

▶ For clothing items, see page 135.

▶ For food items, see page 89.

▶ For souvenirs, see page 133.

You May Hear...

Deseja alguma coisa? deh-zay-zuh ahl-goo-muh koy-zuh	Would you like something?
Um momento. oong moo-mehn-too	One moment.
O que é que deseja? oo kee eh keh deh-zay-zsuh	What would you like?
Mais alguma coisa? meyez ahl-goo-muh koy-zuh	Anything else?

Preferences

I'd like something...	**Queria uma coisa...** keh-ree-uh oo-muh koy-zuh...
– cheap/expensive	– **barato/caro** buh-rah-too/kah-roo
– larger/smaller	– **maior/mais pequena [menor]** meye-awr/ meyez peh-keh-nuh [mee-nawr]
– from this region	– **desta região** dehs-tuh ree-zsee-ohm
Is it real?	**É verdadeiro?** eh vehr-duh-day-roo
Could you show me *this/that*?	**Podia mostrar-me *este/esse*?** poo-dee-uh moos-trahr-meh *ehst/ehs*

Decisions

That's not quite what I want.	**Não é bem o que quero.** nohm eh beng oo keh <u>keh</u>·roo
No, I don't like it.	**Não, não gosto.** nohm nohm <u>gaw</u>·stoo
It's too expensive.	**É caro demais.** eh <u>kah</u>·roo deh·<u>meyez</u>
I have to think about it.	**Tenho que pensar nisto.** <u>tay</u>·nyoo keh pehn·<u>sahr</u> <u>nee</u>·stoo
I'll take it.	**Levo.** <u>leh</u>·voo

Bargaining

That's too much.	**Isso é muito.** <u>ee</u>·soo eh <u>mooee</u>·too
I'll give you…	**Vou dar-lhe…** vau <u>dahr</u>·lyeh…
I only have…*euros/reais*.	**Só tenho…*euros/reais*.** saw <u>teh</u>·nyoo… <u>eeoo</u>·rooz/rree·<u>eyez</u>
Is that your best price?	**É o preço melhor que me pode dar?** eh oo <u>preh</u>·soo mee·<u>lyawr</u> keh meh pawd dahr
Can you give me a discount?	**Pode-me dar um desconto?** <u>pawd</u>·meh dahr oong dehs·<u>kaun</u>·too

▶ For numbers, see page 177.

Paying

How much?	**Quanto é?** <u>kwuhn</u>·too eh
I'll pay…	**Pago…** <u>pah</u>·goo…
– in cash	**– a dinheiro** uh dee·<u>nyay</u>·roo
– by credit card	**– com o cartão de crédito** kaum oo kuhr·<u>tohm</u> deh <u>kreh</u>·dee·too
– by traveler's check [cheque]	**– com livro de cheques** kaum <u>lee</u>·vroo deh <u>sheh</u>·kehz
A receipt, please.	**Um recibo, se faz favor.** oong reh·<u>see</u>·boo seh fahz fuh·<u>vaur</u>

i In Portugal and Brazil, international credit cards are generally accepted. The most commonly used cards are Visa™, American Express®, Europay/Mastercard™, JCB and Maestro®. In some small villages and towns cash may still be the only form of currency accepted.

You May Hear...

Como deseja pagar? kau·moo deh·<u>zay</u>·zsuh puh·<u>gahr</u>	How are you paying?
Esta transacção não foi autorizada. <u>eh</u>·stuh truhn·suh·<u>sohm</u> nohm foy ahoo·too·ree·<u>zah</u>·thuh	This transaction was not authorized.
Posso usar outra forma de identificação? <u>paw</u>·soo oo·<u>zahr</u> <u>au</u>·truh <u>fawr</u>·muh deh ee·dehn·tee·fee·kuh·<u>sohm</u>	May I use another form of identification?
Só a dinheiro, por favor. saw uh dee·<u>nyay</u>·roo poor fuh·<u>vaur</u>	Cash only, please.
Não tem troco [trocado]? nohm teng <u>trau</u>·koo [<u>trau</u>·<u>kah</u>·doo]	Do you have any smaller bills?

Complaints

I'd like...	**Queria...** keh·<u>ree</u>·uh...
– to exchange this	– **trocar isto** troo·<u>kahr</u> <u>ee</u>·stoo
– to return this	– **retornar isto** ree·tawrr·<u>nahr</u> <u>ee</u>·stoo
– a refund	– **um reembolso** oong ree·eng·<u>baul</u>·soo
– to see the manager	– **falar com o gerente** ♂ **/a gerente** ♀ fuh·<u>lahr</u> kaum oo zseh·<u>rehnt</u> ♂ /uh zseh·<u>rehnt</u> ♀

Souvenirs

bottle of wine	**a garrafa de vinho** uh guh·<u>rrah</u>·fuh deh <u>vee</u>·nyoo
box of chocolates	**a caixa de chocolates** uh <u>keye</u>·shuh deh shoo·koo·<u>lah</u>·tehz
calendar	**o calendário** oo kuh·lehn·<u>dah</u>·ree·oo
postcards	**postais** pooz·<u>teyez</u>
scarf	**o lenço** oo <u>lehn</u>·soo
souvenir guide	**o guia turístico** oo <u>gee</u>·uh too·<u>ree</u>·stee·koo
T-shirt	**a camiseta** uh kuh·mee·<u>seh</u>·tuh
toy/game	**o _brinquedo/jogo_** oo _breeng·<u>keh</u>·thoo/<u>zsaw</u>·goo_
wine	**o vinho** oo <u>vee</u>·nyoo
Can I see _this/that_?	**Posso ver _este/esse_?** <u>paw</u>·soo vehr _ehst/ eh·seh_
It's the one in the _window/display case._	**É aquele na _janela/caixa de vidro._** eh uh·<u>kehl</u> nuh _zsuh·<u>neh</u>·luh/<u>keye</u>·shuh deh <u>vee</u>·droo_

I'd like...	Queria... keh·ree·uh...
– a battery	– uma pilha oo·muh pee·lyuh
– a bracelet	– uma pulseira oo·muh pool·say·ruh
– a brooch	– um broche oong brawsh
– earrings	– ums brincos oongs breeng·kooz
– a necklace	– um colar oong koo·lahr
– a ring	– um anel oong uh·nehl
– a watch	– um relógio de pulso oong reh·loy·zsoo deh pool·soo
– copper	– cobre kaw·breh
– crystal	– cristal kree·stahl
– diamonds	– brilhantes bree·lyuhntz
– white/yellow gold	– ouro branco/amarelo au·roo bruhn·kool/ uh·muh·reh·loo
– pearls	– pérolas peh·roo·luhz
– pewter	– peltre pehl·treh
– platinum	– platina plah·tee·nuh
– sterling silver	– prata prah·tuh
Is this real?	É verdadeiro? eh vehr·duh·day·roo
Can you engrave it?	Pode gravá-lo? pawd gruh·vah·loo

Souvenirs you might want to take home from Portugal include pottery leather goods, tiles and copperware, especially the famous **cataplana**. Wooden painted roosters (**galos de barcelos**) also make great souvenirs as they are a national symbol. And don't forget some of the famous **Vinho do Porto**, Port wine.

Popular Brazilian souvenirs include antique furniture, baskets, coffee, dolls in regional costumes, embroidery, Indian crafts, jacaranda-wood salad bowls and trays and tapestries.

Afro-Brazilian musical instruments provide alternative ideas as presents. Some examples are **berimbau** (stretched metal strip, played with a stick), **bongô** (bongo drums) and **atabaque** (another type of drum).

Antiques

How old is this?	**Qual é a data disto?** kwahl eh uh <u>dah</u>·tuh <u>dee</u>·stoo
Do you have anything from the…period?	**Tem alguma coisa do período…?** teng ahl·<u>goo</u>·muh <u>koy</u>·zuh thoo peh·ree·<u>oo</u>·thoo…
Do I have to fill out any forms?	**Tenho que completar qualquer formas?** <u>teh</u>·nyoo keh kaum·pleh·<u>tahr</u> kwahl·<u>kehr</u> <u>fawr</u>·muhz
Is there a certificate of authenticity?	**Há um certificado de autenticidade?** ah oong sehr·tee·fee·<u>kah</u>·thoo deh aw·tehn·tee·see·<u>dahd</u>

Clothing

I'd like…	**Queria…** keh·<u>ree</u>·uh…
Can I try this on?	**Posso provar isto?** <u>paw</u>·soo proo·<u>vahr</u> <u>ee</u>·stoo
It doesn't fit.	**Não me serve.** nohm meh sehrv
It's too…	**É muito…** eh <u>mooee</u>·too…
– big	– **grande** grawnd
– small	– **pequeno** ♂ **/pequena** ♀ peh·<u>kehn</u>·oo ♂ / peh·<u>kehn</u>·uh ♀
– short	– **curto** ♂ **/curta** ♀ <u>koor</u>·too ♂ /<u>koor</u>·tuh ♀
– long	– **comprido** ♂ **/comprida** ♀ kaum·<u>pree</u>·doo ♂ /kaum·<u>pree</u>·duh ♀
Do you have this in size…?	**Tem isto no tamanho…?** teng <u>ee</u>·stoo noo tuh·<u>muh</u>·nyoo…

Do you have this in a *bigger/smaller* size?	**Tem isto num tamanho *maior/mais pequeno* [*menor*]?** teng <u>ee</u>·stoo noong tuh·<u>muh</u>·nyoo meye·<u>awr</u>/ meyez peh·<u>kehn</u>·oo[<u>mee</u>·nor]

▶ For numbers, see page 177.

You May See...

roupa de homem	men's clothing
roupa de senhora	women's clothing
roupa de crianças	children's clothing

Color

I'd like something...	**Queria algo...** keh·<u>ree</u>·uh <u>ahl</u>·goo...
– beige	**– em beige [bege]** eng <u>bay</u>·zseh [<u>bay</u>·zseh]
– black	**– em preto** eng <u>preh</u>·too
– blue	**– em azul** eng uh·<u>zool</u>
– brown	**– em castanho [marrom]** eng kuhz·<u>tay</u>·nyoo [muh·<u>rraum</u>]
– green	**– em verde** eng vehrd
– gray	**– em cinzento [cinza]** eng seeng·<u>zehn</u>·too [<u>seen</u>·zuh]
– orange	**– em cor-de-laranja** eng kaur deh luh·<u>ruhn</u>·zsuh
– pink	**– em cor-de-rosa** eng kaur deh <u>raw</u>·zuh
– purple	**– em roxo** eng <u>rau</u>·shoo
– red	**– em vermelho** eng vehr·<u>meh</u>·lyoo
– white	**– em branco** eng <u>bruhn</u>·koo
– yellow	**– em amarelo** eng uh·meh·<u>reh</u>·loo

Clothes and Accessories

backpack	**a mochila** uh moo·<u>shee</u>·luh
belt	**o cinto** oo <u>seen</u>·too
bikini	**o bikini [biquini]** oo bee·<u>kee</u>·nee [bee·<u>kee</u>·nee]
blouse	**a blusa** uh <u>bloo</u>·zuh
bra	**o soutien [sutiã]** oo soot·ee·<u>ehn</u> [soo·tee·<u>uh</u>]
briefs [underpants]	**as calcinhas** uhz kahl·<u>see</u>·nyuhz
coat	**o casaco comprido** oo kuh·<u>zah</u>·koo kaum·<u>pree</u>·thoo
dress	**o vestido** oo vehs·<u>tee</u>·thoo
hat	**o chapéu** oo shuh·<u>pehoo</u>
jacket	**o casaco curto** oo kuh·<u>zah</u>·koo <u>koor</u>·too
jeans	**as calças de ganga** uhz <u>kahl</u>·suhz deh <u>guhn</u>·guh
pants [trousers]	**as calças** uhz <u>kahl</u>·suhz
pantyhose [tights]	**o collant** oo koo·<u>luhnt</u>
purse [handbag]	**a mala de mão [bolsa]** uh <u>mah</u>·luh deh mohm [<u>baul</u>·sah]
raincoat	**a gabardine** uh guh·buhr·<u>deen</u>
scarf	**o lenço de pescoço** oo <u>lehn</u>·soo deh pehz·<u>kau</u>·soo
shirt	**a camisa** uh kuh·<u>mee</u>·zuh
shorts	**os calções** ooz kahl·<u>soingz</u>
skirt	**a saia** uh <u>seye</u>·uh
socks	**as peúgas [meias curtas]** uhz peh·<u>oo</u>·guhz [<u>may</u>·uhz <u>koor</u>·tuhz]
suit	**o fato [terno]** oo <u>fah</u>·too [<u>tehr</u>·noo]
sunglasses	**os óculos de sol** ooz <u>aw</u>·koo·looz deh sawl
sweater	**a camisola [o suéter]** uh kuh·mee·<u>zaw</u>·luh [oo <u>sweh</u>·tur]

sweatshirt	**o sweatshirt [a blusa de moleton]** oo sweht-shurt [uh bloo-zuh deh mool-ee-tawn]
swimming trunks	**os calções de banho** ooz kahl-soingz deh buh-nyoo
swimsuit	**o fato [maiô] de banho** oo fah-too [meye-au] deh buh-nyoo
T-shirt	**a camiseta/T-shirt** uh kuh-mee-seh-tuh/tee-shurt
tie	**gravata** gruh-vah-tuh
underwear	**roupa interior** rau-puh eeng-teh-ree-aur

Fabric

I'd like...	**Queria...** keh-ree-uh...
– cotton	**– algodão** ahl-goo-dohm
– denim	**– ganga [brim]** guhn-guh [breeng]
– lace	**– renda** rehn-duh
– leather	**– cabedal [couro]** kuh-beh-dahl [kau-roo]
– linen	**– linho** lee-nyoo
– silk	**– seda** seh-thuh
– wool	**– lã** luh
Is it machine washable?	**Isto é para lavar na máquina?** ee-stoo eh puh-ruh luh-vahr nuh mah-kee-nuh

Shoes

I'd like a pair of...	**Queria um par de...** keh-ree-uh oong pahr deh...
– *high-heeled/flat* shoes	**– sapatos *altos/baixos*** suh-pah-tooz *ahl-tooz/beye-shooz*
– boots	**– botas** baw-tuhz
– loafers	**– mandriões** muhn-dree-oingz

– sandals	– **sandálias** suhn·dah·lee·uhz
– shoes	– **sapatos** suh·pah·tooz
– slippers	– **chinelas [pantufas]** shee·neh·luhz [puhn·too·fuhz]
– sneakers	– **sapatos de ténis [tênis]** suh·pah·tooz deh teh·neez [tehn·ehz]
In size...	**No tamanho...** noo tuh·muh·nyoo...

▶ For numbers, see page 177.

Sizes

small (S)	**pequeno** peh·keh·noo
medium (M)	**medio** meh·dee·oo
large (L)	**grande** gruhnd
extra large (XL)	**extra grande** ay·struh gruhnd
petite	**pequeno** peh·keh·noo
plus size	**tamanho de fator positivo** tuh·muh·nyoo deh fah·taur poo·see·tee·voo

Newsstand and Tobacconist

Do you sell English-language newspapers?	**Vende jornais em inglês?** vehn·deh zsoor·neyez eng eeng·lehz
I'd like...	**Queria...** keh·ree·uh...
– candy [sweets]	– **rebuçados [balas]** reh·boo·sah·dooz [bah·luhz]
– chewing gum	– **uma pastilha elástica [goma de mascar]** oo·muh puhz·tee·lyuh ee·lah·stee·kuh [gau·muh deh muhz·kahr]
– a cigar	– **um charuto** oong shuh·roo·too

I'd like...	**Queria...** keh·<u>ree</u>·uh...
– a *pack/carton* of cigarettes	– **um *maço/pacote* de cigarros** oong <u>mah·soo</u>/puh·<u>kaut</u> deh see·<u>gah</u>·rrooz
– a lighter	– **um isqueiro** oong ees·<u>kay</u>·roo
– a magazine	– **uma revista** <u>oo</u>·muh reh·<u>vee</u>·stuh
– matches	– **fósforos** <u>fawz</u>·fuh·rooz
– a newspaper	– **um jornal** oong zsoorr·<u>nahl</u>
– a postcard	– **um postal** oong poo·<u>stahl</u>
– a *road/town* map of...	– **um mapa *do povo/da cidade* de...** oong <u>mah</u>·puh doo <u>pau·voo</u>/deh see·<u>dahd</u> deh...
– stamps	– **selos** <u>seh</u>·looz

Photography

I'd like...	**Queria...** keh·<u>ree</u>·uh...
– a battery	– **uma pilha** <u>oo</u>·muh <u>pee</u>·lyuh
– digital prints	– **impressões digitais** eem·preh·<u>soingz</u> deh·zseh·<u>teyez</u>
– a memory card	– **cartão de memória** kuhr·<u>tohm</u> deh meh·<u>maw</u>·ree·uh
I'm looking for a(n)... camera.	**Estou à procura de [procurando] uma máquina fotográfica...** ee·<u>stawoo</u> ah praw·<u>koo</u>·ruh deh [praw·koo·<u>ruhn</u>·doo] <u>oo</u>·muh <u>mah</u>·kee·nuh faw·too·<u>grah</u>·fee·kuh...
– automatic	– **automática** <u>ahoo</u>·too·<u>mah</u>·tee·kuh
– digital	– **digital** deh·zseh·<u>tahl</u>
– disposable	– **descartável** dehz·kuhr·<u>tah</u>·vehl
Can I print digital photos here?	**Posso imprimir fotos digitais aqui?** <u>paw</u>·soo eem·pree·<u>meer</u> <u>faw</u>·tooz deh·zeh·<u>teyez</u> uh·<u>kee</u>

Sports and Leisure

Essential

When's the game?	**Quando é o jogo?** <u>kwuhn</u>·doo eh o <u>zsau</u>·goo
Where's…?	**Onde é…** aund eh…
– the beach	– **a praia** uh <u>preye</u>·uh
– the park	– **o parque** oo <u>pahr</u>·keh
– the pool	– **a piscina** uh pee·<u>see</u>·nuh
Is it safe to swim here?	**Pode-se nadar aqui sem perigo?** pawd seh nuh·<u>dahr</u> uh·<u>kee</u> sehn peh·<u>ree</u>·goo
Can I rent [hire] golf clubs?	**Posso alugar tacos?** <u>paw</u>·soo uh·loo·<u>gahr</u> <u>tah</u>·kooz
How much per hour?	**Qual é a tarifa por hora?** kwahl eh uh tuh·<u>ree</u>·fuh poor <u>aw</u>·ruh
How far is it to…?	**A que distância fica…?** uh keh dee·<u>stuhn</u>·see·uh <u>fee</u>·kuh…
Can you show me on the map?	**Pode indicar-me no mapa?** pawd een·dee·<u>kahr</u>·meh noo <u>mah</u>·puh

Spectator Sports

When's…	**Quando é…** <u>kwuhn</u>·doo eh…
– the basketball game	– **o jogo de basquetebol** oo <u>zsau</u>·goo deh <u>bah</u>·skeht·bawl
– the boxing match	– **a partida de boxe** uh puhr·<u>tee</u>·duh deh bawkz
– the cycling race	– **a corrida de bicicleta** uh koo·<u>ree</u>·thuh deh bee·see·<u>kleht</u>
– the golf tournament	– **o torneio de golfe** oo taur·<u>nay</u>·oo deh gawlf
– the soccer [football] game	– **o jogo de futebol** oo <u>zsau</u>·goo deh <u>foo</u>·teh·bawl

When's...	**Quando é...** kwuhn·doo eh...
– the tennis match	**– a partida de tênis** uh puhr·<u>tee</u>·thuh de <u>teh</u>·neez
– the volleyball game	**– o jogo de voleibol** oo <u>zsau</u>·goo deh vaw·lay·bawl
Which teams are playing?	**Quais são as equipas [os times] que jogam?** kweyez sohm uhz ee·<u>kee</u>·puhz [ooz <u>tee</u>·mehs] keh <u>zsau</u>·gohm
Where's...?	**Onde é...** aund eh...
– the horsetrack	**– a pista de cavalo** uh <u>peez</u>·tuh deh kuh·<u>vah</u>·loo
– the racetrack	**– o hipódromo** oo ee·paw·<u>drau</u>·moo
– the stadium	**– o pavilhão desportivo [esportivo]** oo puh·vee·<u>lyohm</u> dehs·poor·<u>tee</u>·voo [ees·poor·<u>tee</u>·voo]
Where can I place a bet?	**Onde posso colocar uma aposta?** aund <u>paw</u>·soo kaw·loo·<u>kahr</u> <u>oo</u>·muh uh·<u>paws</u>·tuh

Portuguese and Brazilians are avid soccer fans. In Portugal, the teams Porto and Sporting Lisbon attract huge crowds, while Rio boasts Maracanã, the largest soccer stadium in the world.

Participating

Where's…?	**Onde é…?** aund eh…
– the golf course	– **o campo de golfe** oo kuhm·poo deh gawlf
– the gym	– **o clube desportivo [esportivo]** oo kloob dehs·poor·tee·voo [ees·poor·tee·voo]
– the park	– **o parque** oo pahrk
– the tennis courts	– **os campos [as quadras] de ténis** ooz kuhm·pooz [uhz kwah·druhz] deh teh·neez
How much per…?	**Qual é o preço por…?** kwahl eh oo preh·soo poor…
– day	– **dia** dee·uh
– hour	– **hora** aw·ruh
– game	– **jogo** zsau·goo
– round	– **volta** vawl·tuh
Can I rent [hire]…?	**Posso alugar…?** paw·soo uh·loo·gahr…
– golf clubs	– **tacos de golfe** tah·kooz deh gawlf
– equipment	– **o equipamento** oo ee·kee·puh·mehn·too
– a racket	– **uma raquete** oo·muh rah·keht

At the Beach/Pool

Where's *the beach/pool*?	**Onde é a *praia/piscina*?** aund eh uh *preye·uh/pee·see·nuh*
Is there…?	**Há…?** ah…
– a kiddie pool	– **uma piscina para crianças** oo·muh pee·see·nuh puh·ruh kree·uhn·suhs
– an *indoor/outdoor* pool	– **uma piscina *coberta/ao ar livre*** oo·muh pee·see·nuh *koo·behr·tuh/ahoo ahr lee·vreh*
– a lifeguard	– **uma salva-vidas** oo·muh sahl·vuh vee·duhz

Is it safe...?	**É perigoso...?** eh per·ree·<u>gau</u>·zoo...
– to swim	**– para nadar** puh·ruh nuh·<u>dahr</u>
– to dive	**– para mergulhar** <u>puh</u>·ruh mehr·goo·<u>lyahr</u>
– for children	**– para as crianças** <u>puh</u>·ruh uhz kree·<u>uhn</u>·suhs
I want to rent [hire]...	**Quero alugar...** <u>keh</u>·roo uh·loo·<u>gahr</u>...
– a deck chair	**– uma cadeira de encosto** <u>oo</u>·muh kuh·<u>day</u>·ruh deh ehn·<u>kaus</u>·stoo
– diving equipment	**– equipamento para mergulhar** ee·kee·puh·<u>mehn</u>·too <u>puh</u>·ruh mehr·goo·<u>lyahr</u>
– a jet-ski	**– um jet-ski** oong <u>zseht</u>·skee
– a motorboat	**– um barco a motor** oong <u>bahr</u>·koo uh moo·<u>taur</u>
– a rowboat	**– um barco a remos** oong <u>bahr</u>·koo uh <u>reh</u>·mooz
– snorkling equipment	**– equipamento de snorkling** ee·kee·puh·<u>mehn</u>·too de <u>snawr</u>·kleeng
– a surfboard	**– uma prancha de surf** <u>oo</u>·muh <u>pruhn</u>·shuh deh soorf
– a towel	**– uma toalha** <u>oo</u>·muh too·<u>ah</u>·lyuh
– an umbrella	**– um chapéu de sol [guarda sol]** oong shuh·<u>pehoo</u> deh sol [<u>gwahr</u>·duh sawl]
– water skis	**– esquis-aquáticos** eez·<u>keez</u> uh·<u>kwah</u>·tee·kooz
– a windsurfer	**– uma prancha à vela** <u>oo</u>·muh <u>pruhn</u>·shuh ah <u>veh</u>·luh
For...hours.	**Por...horas.** poor...<u>aw</u>·ruhz

▶ For travel with children, see page 155.

 In Portugal, the **Algarve** has beautiful beaches, and the **Alentejo** (Atlantic Coast) is growing in popularity. Beaches in the north (**Caminha**, **Apúlia**, **Furadouro**) are good for surfing.

Brazil is practically synonymous with beaches; **Copacabana** and **Ipanema** in Rio are known the world over. Surfing is popular all along the Brazilian coast, and beach volleyball is also a popular pursuit.

In both Portugal and Brazil, the largest beaches have lifeguards, but look for the following swimming flags: red (swimming forbidden), yellow (swim near the beach), green (safe).

Winter Sports

A lift pass for *a day/ five days*, please.	**Uma passagem de esqui por *um dia/ cinco dias*, por favor.** oo·muh puh·<u>sah</u>·zseng deh ee·<u>skee</u> poor *oong <u>dee</u>·uh/<u>seeng</u>·koo <u>dee</u>·uhz* poor fuh·<u>vaur</u>
I want to rent [hire]…	**Quero alugar…** <u>keh</u>·roo uh·loo·<u>gahr</u>…
– boots	– **botas** <u>baw</u>·tuhz
– a helmet	– **um capacete** oong kuh·puh·<u>seht</u>
– poles	– **polos** <u>pau</u>·looz
– skis	– **esquis** ee·<u>skeez</u>
– a snowboard	– **um snowboard** oong sno·<u>bawrd</u>
– snowshoes	– **sapatos de neve** suh·<u>pah</u>·tooz deh nehv
These are too *big/ small*.	**Estes são muito *grandes/ pequenos*.** <u>ehs</u>·tehz sohm <u>mooee</u>·too *gruhn·dehz/ pee·<u>keh</u>·nooz*
Are there lessons?	**Há lições?** ah lee·<u>soingz</u>
I'm a beginner.	**Sou principiante.** sawoo preen·see·<u>puhnt</u>
I'm experienced.	**Tenho experiência.** <u>teh</u>·nyoo ees·peh·ree·<u>ehn</u>·see·uh
A trail [piste] map, please.	**Um mapa de trilha, por favor.** oong <u>mah</u>·puh deh <u>tree</u>·lyuh poor fuh·<u>vaur</u>

i There is one place in Portugal with temperatures cold enough for skiing; **Serra da Estrela**, Portugal's highest mountain. Dress appropriately, as the weather at the bottom of the mountain (and the rest of Portugal) is not indicative of the freezing temperatures at the top of **Serra da Estrela**. It is not uncommon for temperatures to be thirty to fifty degrees colder at the top!

You May See…

LEVANTA DE ESQUI	drag lift
CARRO DE CABO/GANDOLA	cable car/gondola
CADEIRA LEVANTAMENTO	chair lift
NOVATO	novice
INTERMEDIÁRIO	intermediate
ESPECIALISTA	expert
TRILHA FECHADA	trail [piste] closed

In the Countryside

I'd like a map…	**Queria um mapa…** keh·<u>ree</u>·uh oong <u>mah</u>·puh…
– of this region	– **desta região** <u>deh</u>·stuh reh·zsee·<u>ohm</u>
– of the walking routes	– **de itinerários a pé** deh ee·tee·neh·<u>rah</u>·ree·ooz a peh
– of bike routes	– **de itinerários de bicicleta** deh ee·tee·neh·<u>rah</u>·ree·ooz deh bee·see·<u>kleh</u>·tuh
– of the trails	– **dos caminhos** thooz kuh·<u>mee</u>·nyooz
Is it *easy/difficult*?	**É *fácil/difícil*?** eh <u>fah</u>·seel/dee·<u>fee</u>·seel
Is it *far/steep*?	**É *distante/precipício*?** eh deez·<u>tuhnt</u>/ pree·see·<u>pee</u>·see·oo

146

How far is it to…?	**A que distância fica…** uh keh dee·<u>stuhn</u>·see·uh <u>fee</u>·kuh…
Can you show me on the map?	**Pode indicar-me no mapa?** pawd een·dee·<u>kahr</u>·meh noo <u>mah</u>·puh
I'm lost.	**Estou perdido ♂/perdida ♀.** ee·<u>stawoo</u> pehr·<u>dee</u>·doo ♂/pehr·<u>dee</u>·duh ♀
Where's…?	**Onde é…** aund eh…
– the bridge	**– a ponte** uh paunt
– the cave	**– a caverna** uh kuh·<u>vehr</u>·nuh
– the cliff	**– a falésia** uh fuh·<u>leh</u>·see·uh
– the farm	**– a quinta [fazenda]** uh <u>keen</u>·tuh [fuh·<u>zehn</u>·dah]
– the field	**– o campo** oo <u>kuhm</u>·poo
– the forest	**– a floresta** uh flau·<u>reh</u>·stuh
– the hill	**– a colina** uh koo·<u>lee</u>·nuh
– the lake	**– o lago** oo <u>lah</u>·goo
– the mountain	**– a montanha** uh maun·<u>tah</u>·nyuh
– the nature preserve	**– a reserva natural** uh reh·<u>zehr</u>·vuh nuh·too·<u>rahl</u>
– the overlook [view point]	**– o miradouro** oo mee·ruh·<u>dau</u>·roo
– the park	**– o parque** oo pahrk
– the path	**– o caminho para peões [pedestres]** oo kuh·<u>mee</u>·nyoo <u>puh</u>·ruh pee·<u>oingz</u> [peh·<u>dehs</u>·trehz]
– the peak	**– o pico** oo <u>pee</u>·koo
– the pond	**– a lagoa** uh luh·<u>gaw</u>·uh
– the river	**– o rio** oo <u>rree</u>·oo
– the sea	**– o mar** oo mahr
– the valley	**– o vale** oo vahl

Where's...?	**Onde é...** aund eh...
– the vineyard	**– a vinha** uh <u>vee</u>·nyuh
– the waterfall	**– a cascata** uh kuhz·<u>kah</u>·tuh

Culture and Nightlife

Essential

What is there to do in the evenings?	**O que há para se fazer à noite?** oo keh ah <u>puh</u>·ruh seh fuh·<u>zehr</u> ah noyt
Do you have a program of events?	**Tem um programa dos espectáculos?** teng oong proo·<u>gruh</u>·muh dooz ee·spehk·<u>tah</u>·koo·looz
What's playing at the movies [cinema] tonight?	**O que há no cinema hoje à noite?** oo kee ah noo see·<u>neh</u>·muh auzseh ah noyt
Where's...?	**Onde é...** aund eh...
– the downtown area	**– o centro** oo <u>sehn</u>·troo
– the bar	**– o bar** oo bar
– the dance club	**– a discoteca** uh deez·koo·<u>teh</u>·kuh
Is there a cover charge?	**É preciso pagar entrada [ingresso]?** eh preh·<u>see</u>·zoo puh·<u>gahr</u> ehn·<u>trah</u>·duh [een·<u>greh</u>·soo]

i **Carnaval** is widely celebrated both in Portugal and Brazil. A time of lavish celebration before Lent, **Carnaval** begins four days before Ash Wednesday, and ends with the famous "Fat Tuesday" celebration. Look for parades on the streets and carnival balls (**bailes carnavalescos**). The famed **Carnaval do Rio** sees the spectacularly colorful competition between the various samba schools in their parade through the streets of Rio de Janiero.

Samba and bossa nova are the dance styles best known
abroad; but regional rhythms like **pagode**, **lambada**, **frevo**,
forró, **maracatu**, **baião**, **carimbó** and **bumba-meu boi**, with
their mixture of African, Indian, and European influences, are
also very popular with locals and tourists.

Entertainment

Can you recommend…?	**Pode recomendar-me…?** pawd reh·koo·mehn·<u>dahr</u>·meh…
– a concert	**– um concerto** oong kaun·<u>sehr</u>·too
– a movie	**– um filme** oong <u>feel</u>·meh
– an opera	**– uma ópera** oo·muh <u>aw</u>·peh·ruh
– a play	**– um teatro** oong tee·<u>ah</u>·troo
When does it *start/ end*?	**A que horas *começa/ acaba*?** uh kee <u>aw</u>·ruhz koo·<u>meh</u>·suh/uh·<u>kah</u>·buh
What's the dress code?	**O que é o código de vestido?** oo kee eh oo <u>kaw</u>·dee·goo deh vehs·<u>tee</u>·thoo
I like…	**Gosto de…** <u>gaws</u>·too deh…
– classical music	**– música clássica** <u>moo</u>·zee·kuh <u>klah</u>·see·kuh
– folk music	**– música popular** <u>moo</u>·zee·kuh poo·poo·<u>lahr</u>
– jazz	**– jazz** zsahz
– pop music	**– pop** pawp
– rap	**– rap** rahp

▶ For ticketing, see page 21.

A popular evening activity in Portugal is a visit to a **casa de
fados** (house of blues), an intimate, late-night restaurant
where your meal is accompanied by the melodies of the **fado**,
the national folk song.

Local papers and weekly entertainment guides—such as **Sete** in Portugal and **Veja** in Brazil—will tell you what's on. Regional booklets (**vejinha**) are also useful in Brazil.

You May Hear...

Desligue seus telefones celulares, por favor. dehz·<u>lee</u>·geh sehooz tehl·<u>fawnz</u> sehl·oo·<u>lahrz</u> poor fuh·<u>vaur</u>	Turn off your cell [mobile] phones, please.

Nightlife

What is there to do in the evenings?	**O que há para se fazer à noite?** oo keh ah <u>puh</u>·ruh seh fuh·<u>zehr</u> ah noyt
Can you recommend...?	**Pode recomendar-me...?** pawd reh·koo·mehn·<u>dahr</u>·meh...
– a bar	**– um bar** oong bar
– a casino	**– um casino** oong kuh·<u>see</u>·noo
– a dance club	**– uma discoteca** <u>oo</u>·muh dee·skoo·<u>teh</u>·kuh
– a gay club	**– um clube gay** oong kloob gay
– a jazz club	**– um clube de jazz** oong kloob deh zsahz
Is there live music?	**Há música ao vivo?** ah <u>moo</u>·zee·kuh ahoo <u>vee</u>·voo
How do I get there?	**Como é que vou até lá?** <u>kau</u>·moo eh keh vauoo uh·<u>teh</u> lah
Is there a cover charge?	**É preciso pagar entrada [ingresso]?** eh preh·<u>see</u>·zoo puh·<u>gahr</u> ehn·<u>trah</u>·duh [een·<u>greh</u>·soo]
Let's go dancing.	**Vamos dançar.** <u>vuh</u>·mooz duhn·<u>sahr</u>

i Portugal offers the usual range of nightclubs along the coast; most don't begin to get lively until around midnight.

Special Needs

Essential

I'm here on business.	**Estou aqui de negócio.** ee·<u>stawoo</u> uh·<u>kee</u> deh neh·<u>gaw</u>·see·oo
Here's my business card.	**Tome o meu cartão.** <u>taw</u>·meh oo meeoo kuhr·<u>tohm</u>
Can I have your card?	**Posso ter a sua cartão?** <u>paw</u>·soo tehr a <u>soo</u>·uh kuhr·<u>tohm</u>
I have a meeting with...	**Tenho um apontamento com...** <u>tay</u>·nyoo oong uh·paun·tuh·<u>mehn</u>·too kaum...
Where's...?	**Onde é...** aund eh...
– the business center	– **o centro de negócio** oo <u>sehn</u>·troo deh neh·<u>gaw</u>·see·oo
– the convention hall	– **o lugar de convenção** oo loo·<u>gahr</u> deh kaun·vehn·<u>sohm</u>
– the meeting room	– **o lugar de reunião** oo loo·<u>garh</u> deh rree·oo·nee·<u>ohm</u>

Business Communication

I'm here to attend...	**Estou aqui para participar...** ee·<u>stawoo</u> uh·<u>kee</u> <u>puh</u>·ruh puhr·tee·see·<u>pahr</u>...
– a seminar	– **num seminário** noong seh·mee·<u>nah</u>·ree·oo
– a conference	– **numa conferência** <u>noo</u>·muh kaun·feh·<u>rehn</u>·see·uh
– a meeting	– **numa reunião** <u>noo</u>·muh rree·oo·nee·<u>ohm</u>
My name is...	**Chamo-me... [Meu nome é...]** <u>shuh</u>·moo meh... [mehoo <u>naum</u>·ee eh...]
May I introduce my colleague...	**Posso introduzir o meu colega ♂.../a minha colega ♀...** <u>paw</u>·soo eeng·troo·thoo·<u>zeer</u> oo mehoo koo·<u>leh</u>·guh ♂.../ uh <u>mee</u>·nyuh koo·<u>leh</u>·guh ♀...

I have *a meeting/an appointment* with…	**Tenho *uma reunião/ um apontamento* com…** tay·nyoo *oo·muh rree·oo·nee·<u>ohm</u>/ oong uh·paun·tuh·<u>mehn</u>·too* kaum…
I'm sorry I'm late.	**Desculpa, estou atrasado ♂/atrasada ♀.** dehs·<u>kool</u>·puh ee·<u>stawoo</u> uh·truh·<u>zah</u>·thoo ♂ / uh·truh·<u>zah</u>·thuh ♀
I need an interpreter.	**Preciso de um tradutor.** preh·<u>see</u>·zoo deh oong truh·doo·<u>taur</u>
You can reach me at the…Hotel.	**Podes me encontrar no hotel…** <u>pawd</u>·ehz meh eng·kaun·<u>trahr</u> noo aw·<u>tehl</u>…
I'm here until…	**Estou aqui até…** ee·<u>stawoo</u> uh·<u>kee</u> uh·<u>teh</u>…

Business culture in Portugal respects age and position and holds to strict rules of behavior. Never interrupt a business colleague during a presentation; hand gestures are considered rude and not used to express feelings; appointments are mandatory and lateness unacceptable; eye contact is essential. Do not use high-pressure sales tactics, as aggressive behavior is often seen as offensive.

I need to...	**Preciso de...** preh·see·zoo deh...
– make a call	– **fazer um telefonema** fuh·zehr oong teh·leh·faw·neh·muh
– make a photocopy	– **fazer uma fotocópia** fuh·zehr oo·muh faw·taw·kaw·pee·uh
– send an e-mail	– **enviar um e-mail** eng·vee·ahr oong ee·mehl
– send a fax	– **enviar um fax** ehn·vee·ahr oong fahks
– send a package (overnight)	– **enviar um embrulho (de um dia ao próximo)** ehn·vee·ahr oong eng·broo·lyoo (deh oong dee·uh ahoo praw·see·moo)
It was a pleasure to meet you.	**Muito prazer.** mooee·too pruh·zehr

▶ For internet and communications, see page 52.

You May Hear...

Você tem um apontamento? vaw·seh teng oong uh·paun·tuh·mehn·too	Do you have an appointment?
Com quem? kaum keng	With whom?
Está numa reunião. ee·stah noo·muh ree·oo·nee·ohm	*He/She* is in a meeting.
Um momento, por favor. oong moo·mehn·too poor fuh·vaur	One moment, please.
Asenta-se. uh·sehn·tuh·sheh	Have a seat.
Quer qualquer coisa para beber? kehr kwahl·kehr coy·zuh puh·ruh beh·behr	Would you like something to drink?
Obrigado ♂/**Obrigada** ♀ **por vir.** aw·bree·gah·thoo ♂/aw·bree·gah·thuh ♀ poor veer	Thank you for coming.

Essential

Is there a discount for children?	**Há desconto para crianças?** ah dehs·<u>caun</u>·too puh·ruh kree·<u>uhn</u>·suhs
Can you recommend a babysitter?	**Pode recomendar-me uma babysitter [babá] qualificada?** pawd reh·koo·mehn·<u>dahr</u>·meh <u>oo</u>·muh bay·bee·sit·tur [bah·<u>buh</u>] kwahl·ee·fee·<u>kah</u>·duh
Do you have a child's seat?	**Pode trazer uma cadeirinha de criança?** pawd truh·<u>zehr</u> <u>oo</u>·muh kuh·day·<u>ree</u>·nyuh deh kree·<u>uhn</u>·suh
Where can I change the baby?	**Onde posso mudar o bebé [nenê]?** aund <u>paw</u>·soo moo·<u>dahr</u> oo beh·<u>beh</u> [neh·<u>neh</u>]

Fun with Kids

Can you recommend something for the kids?	**Pode recomendar-me algo próprio para crianças?** pawd reh·koo·mehn·<u>dahr</u>·meh <u>ahl</u>·goo <u>praw</u>·pree·oo puh·ruh kree·<u>uhn</u>·suhs
Where's…?	**Onde é…** aund eh…
– the amusement park	– **o parque de divertimento** oo <u>pahr</u>·keh deh dee·vehr·tee·<u>mehn</u>·too
– the arcade	– **o salão de jogos** oo suh·<u>lohm</u> deh <u>zsaw</u>·gooz
– the kiddie [paddling] pool	– **a piscina de bebés [nenês]** uh pee·<u>see</u>·nuh deh beh·<u>behz</u> [neh·<u>nehz</u>]
– the park	– **o parque** oo pahrk
– the playground	– **o parque de recreio [playground]** oo pahrk deh reh·<u>kray</u>·oo [<u>play</u>·graund]
– the zoo	– **o jardim zoológico** oo zsuhr·<u>deem</u> zoo·<u>law</u>·zsee·koo

Are kids allowed?	**Crianças são permitidas?** kree-<u>uhn</u>-suhz sohm pehr-mee-<u>tee</u>-thuhz
Is it safe for kids?	**É seguro para as crianças?** eh seh-<u>goo</u>-roo <u>puh</u>-ruh uhz kree-<u>uhn</u>-suhs
Is it suitable for... year olds?	**Será bom para crianças com... anos?** seh-<u>rah</u> bohng <u>puh</u>-ruh kree-<u>uhn</u>-suhz kaum...<u>uh</u>-nooz

▶ For numbers, see page 177.

You May Hear...

Que giro! keh <u>zsee</u>-roo	How cute!
O que é o nome *d'ele/d'ela*? oo kee eh oo <u>nau</u>-meh *dehl/<u>deh</u>-luh*	What's *his/her* name?
Quantos anos tem *ele/ela*? <u>kwuh</u>-tooz <u>uh</u>-nooz teng *ehl/<u>eh</u>-luh*	How old is *he/she*?

Basic Needs for Kids

Do you have...?	**Tem...?** teng...
– a baby bottle	– **um bribrom** oong bree-<u>brohng</u>
– baby wipes	– **os toalhetes de limpeza para o bebé [nenê]** ooz too-ah-<u>lyehtz</u> deh leem-<u>peh</u>-zuh <u>puh</u>-ruh oo beh-<u>beh</u> [neh-<u>neh</u>]

– a car seat	– **um assento de carro** oong uh-<u>sehn</u>-too deh <u>kah</u>-rroo
– a children's *menu/portion*	– **uma *emental/porção* de criança** oo-muh ee-<u>mehn</u>-tuh/poor-<u>sohm</u> deh kree-<u>uhn</u>-suh
– a child's seat	– **uma cadeirinha de criança** <u>oo</u>-muh kuh-day-ree-<u>ree</u>-nyuh deh kree-<u>uhn</u>-suh
– a crib	– **uma cama de bebé [nenê]** <u>oo</u>-muh <u>kuh</u>-muh deh beh-<u>beh</u> [neh-<u>neh</u>]
– diapers [nappies]	– **as fraldas** uhz <u>frahl</u>-duhz
– formula	– **fórmula de bebê [nenê]** <u>fawr</u>-moo-luh deh beh-<u>beh</u> [neh-<u>neh</u>]
– a pacifier [soother]	– **uma chupeta** <u>oo</u>-muh shoo-<u>peh</u>-tuh
– a playpen	– **um cercado para crianças** oong sehr-<u>kah</u>-thoo puh-ruh kree-<u>uhn</u>-suhz
– a stroller [pushchair]	– **um caminhante de bebê [nenê]** oong kuh-mee-<u>nyuhnt</u> deh beh-<u>beh</u> [neh-<u>neh</u>]
Can I breastfeed the baby here?	**Posso amamentar o bebê [nenê] aqui?** <u>paw</u>-soo uh-muh-mehn-<u>tahr</u> oo beh-<u>beh</u> [neh-<u>neh</u>] uh-<u>kee</u>
Where can I change the baby?	**Onde posso mudar o bebé [nenê]?** aund <u>paw</u>-soo moo-<u>thahr</u> oo beh-<u>beh</u> [neh-<u>neh</u>]

▶ For dining with kids, see page 67.

Babysitting

Can you recommend a reliable babsitter?	**Pode recomendar-me uma babysitter [babá] qualificada?** pawd reh-koo-mehn-<u>dahr</u>-meh <u>oo</u>-muh bay-bee-sit-tur [bah-<u>bah</u>] kwah-lee-fee-<u>kah</u>-thuh
What's the charge?	**Qual é o preço?** kwahl eh oo <u>preh</u>-soo
I'll be back by…	**Volto ás…** <u>vawl</u>-too ahz…

▶ For time, see page 179.

I can be reached at…	**Podes me encontrar…** <u>paw</u>-dehz meh eng-kaun-<u>trahr</u>…

Health and Emergency —————————

Can you recommend a pediatrician?	**Pode recomendar um pediatra?** pawd reh-kau-mehn-<u>dahr</u> oong pee-dee-<u>ah</u>-truh
My child is allergic to…	**A minha criança é alérgico ♂/alérgica ♀ a…** uh <u>mee</u>-nyuh kree-<u>uhn</u>-suh eh uh-<u>lehr</u>-gee-koo ♂/uh-<u>lehr</u>-gee-kuh ♀ uh…
My son/daughter is missing.	**Desapareceu o meu filho/a minha filha.** deh-zuh-puh-ruh-<u>seoo</u> oo mehoo <u>fee</u>-lyoo/uh <u>mee</u>-nyuh <u>fee</u>-lyuh
Have you seen a *boy/girl*?	**Viu um menino/uma menina?** veeoo oong meh-<u>nee</u>-noo/<u>oo</u>-muh meh-<u>nee</u>-nuh

▶ For food items, see page 89.

▶ For health, see page 163.

▶ For police, see page 161.

For the Disabled

Essential

Is there…?	**Há…?** ah…
– access for the disabled	**– acesso para deficientes físicos** uh-<u>seh</u>-soo <u>puh</u>-ruh deh-fee-see-<u>ehntz</u> <u>fee</u>-see-kooz
– a wheelchair ramp	**– uma rampa de cadeira de rodas** <u>oo</u>-muh <u>ruhm</u>-puh deh kuh-<u>day</u>-ruh deh <u>raw</u>-thuhz
– a handicapped-[disabled-] accessible toilet	**– um banheiro limitou-acessível** oong bah-<u>nyay</u>-roo lee-mee-<u>tau</u> uh-seh-<u>see</u>-vehl

I need...	**Preciso de...** preh·<u>see</u>·zoo deh...
– assistance	– **assistência** uh·see·<u>stehn</u>·see·uh
– an elevator [lift]	– **um elevador** oong eh·leh·vuh·<u>daur</u>
– a ground–floor room	– **um quarto no primeiro andar** oong <u>kwahr</u>·too noo pree·<u>may</u>·roo uhn·<u>dahr</u>

Getting Help

I'm disabled.	**Sou deficiente.** sawoo deh·fee·see·<u>ehnt</u>
I'm deaf.	**Sou surdo.** sawoo <u>soor</u>·doo
I'm *visually/hearing* impaired.	**Sou prejudicado *visualmente/ de audiçao.*** sawoo preh·zsoo·dee·<u>kah</u>·thoo *vee·zoo·ahl·<u>mehnt</u>/ deh au·dee·<u>sohm</u>*
I'm unable to *walk far/use the stairs.*	**Não posso *caminhar longe/usar as escadas.*** nohm <u>paw</u>·soo kuh·mee·<u>nyahr</u> <u>laun</u>·zseh/oo·<u>zahr</u> uhz ee·<u>skah</u>·thuhz
Can I bring my wheelchair?	**Posso trazer a minha cadeira de rodas?** <u>paw</u>·soo truh·<u>zehr</u> uh <u>mee</u>·nyuh kuh·<u>day</u>·ruh deh <u>raw</u>·duhz
Are guide dogs permitted?	**Os cães de guia são permitidos?** ooz kengs de <u>gee</u>·uh sohm pehr·mee·<u>tee</u>·dooz
Can you help me?	**Pode ajudar-me?** pawd uh·zsoo·<u>dahr</u>·meh
Please *open/hold* the door.	**Por favor *abra/ segure* a porta.** poor fuh·<u>vaur</u> *<u>ah</u>·bruh/ seh·<u>goo</u>·reh* uh <u>pawr</u>·tuh

159

▼ Resources

Emergencies

Essential

Help!	**Socorro!** soo·<u>kau</u>·rroo
Go away!	**Vá-se embora!** <u>vah</u>·seh ehng·<u>baw</u>·ruh
Call the police!	**Chame a polícia!** <u>shuh</u>·meh uh poo·<u>lee</u>·see·uh
Stop thief!	**Pára ladrão!** <u>pah</u>·ruh luh·<u>drohm</u>
Get a doctor!	**Chame um médico!** <u>shuh</u>·meh oong <u>meh</u>·dee·koo
Fire!	**Fogo!** <u>fau</u>·goo
I'm lost.	**Estou perdido** ♂ **/perdida** ♀. ee·<u>stawoo</u> pehr·<u>dee</u>·thoo ♂/pehr·<u>dee</u>·thuh ♀
Can you help me?	**Pode ajudar-me?** pawd uh·zsoo·<u>dahr</u>·meh

Police

Essential

Call the police!	**Chame a polícia!** <u>shuh</u>·meh uh poo·<u>lee</u>·see·uh
Where's the police station?	**Onde é a esquadra [delegacia] da polícia?** aund eh uh ee·<u>skwahr</u>·duh [deh·leh·guh·<u>see</u>·uh] thuh poo·<u>lee</u>·see·uh
There has been an *accident/attack*.	**Houve um *accidente/ataque*.** <u>auoo</u>·veh oong uh·see·<u>dehnt</u>/uh·<u>tah</u>·keh
My son/daughter is missing.	**Desapareceu *o meu filho/a minha filha*.** deh·zuh·puh·ruh·<u>seoo</u> oo mehoo <u>fee</u>·lyoo/uh <u>mee</u>·nyuh <u>fee</u>·lyuh
I need...	**Preciso de...** preh·<u>see</u>·zoo deh...
– an interpreter	**– um tradutor** oong truh·doo·<u>taur</u>

I need...	**Preciso de...** preh·<u>see</u>·zoo deh...
– to contact my lawyer	– **contatar o meu advogado.** kaun·tuh·<u>tahr</u> oo mehoo uhd·voo·<u>gah</u>·thoo
– to make a phone call	– **fazer um telefonema** fuh·<u>zehr</u> oong teh·leh·foo·<u>neh</u>·muh
I'm innocent.	**Sou inocente.** sawoo ee·naw·<u>sehnt</u>

You May Hear...

Preencha esta forma. pree·<u>eng</u>·sheh <u>eh</u>·stuh <u>fawr</u>·muh	Fill out this form.
Sua identificação, por favor. <u>soo</u>·uh ee·dehnt·tee·fee·kuh·<u>sohm</u> por fuh·<u>vaur</u>	Your identification, please.
Quando/Onde **é que foi?** <u>kwuhn</u>·doo/aund eh keh foy	*When/Where* did it happen?
Como é que se aparece? <u>kau</u>·moo eh keh seh uh·puh·<u>reh</u>·seh	What does *he/she* look like?

Lost Property and Theft —————

I want to report...	**Quero reportar...** <u>keh</u>·roo reh·paur·<u>tahr</u>...
– a mugging	– **um assalto** oong uh·<u>sahl</u>·too
– a rape	– **uma violação [um estupro]** <u>oo</u>·muh vee·au·luh·<u>sohm</u> [oong ee·<u>stoo</u>·proo]
– a theft	– **um roubo** oong <u>rau</u>·boo
I've been robbed.	**Fui roubado** ♂/**rubada** ♀. fooee raw·<u>bah</u>·thoo ♂/raw·<u>bah</u>·thuh ♀
I've been mugged.	**Fui assaltado** ♂/**assaltada** ♀. fooee uh·sahl·<u>tah</u>·thoo ♂/uh·sahl·<u>tah</u>·duh ♀
I've lost my...	**Perdi...** pehr·<u>thee</u>...

My…has been stolen.	**Roubaram-me…** raw·<u>bah</u>·rohm·meh…
– backpack	**– a mochila** uh moo·<u>sheeh</u>·luh
– bicycle	**– a bicileta** uh bee·see·<u>kleh</u>·tuh
– camera	**– a máquina fotográfica** uh <u>mah</u>·kee·nuh faw·too·<u>grah</u>·fee·kuh
– (rental [hire]) car	**– o carro (alugado)** oo <u>kah</u>·rroo (uh·loo·<u>gah</u>·doo)
– computer	**– o computador** oo kaum·poo·tuh·<u>daur</u>
– credit card	**– os cartão de crédito** ooz kuhr·<u>tohm</u> deh <u>kreh</u>·dee·too
– jewelry	**– as jóias** uhz <u>zsoy</u>·uhz
– money	**– o dinheiro** oo dee·<u>nyay</u>·roo
– passport	**– o passaporte** oo pah·suh·<u>pawrt</u>
– purse [hándbag]	**– a carteira** uh kuhr·<u>tay</u>·truh
– traveler's checks [cheques]	**– os cheques de viagem.** ooz shehkz deh vee·<u>ah</u>·zseng
– wallet	**– a carteira (de documentos)** uh kuhr·<u>tay</u>·ruh (deh doo·koo·<u>mehn</u>·tooz)
I need a police report.	**Preciso de um documento da policia.** preh·<u>see</u>·zoo deh oong thoo·koo·<u>mehn</u>·too duh poo·<u>lee</u>·see·uh

Health

Essential

I'm sick.	**Estou doente.** ee·<u>stawoo</u> doo·<u>ehnt</u>
I need an English-speaking doctor.	**Preciso de um médico que fale inglês.** preh·<u>see</u>·zoo deh oong <u>meh</u>·dee·koo keh <u>fah</u>·leh eeng·<u>lehz</u>
It hurts here.	**Dói-me aqui.** <u>doy</u>·meh uh·<u>kee</u>
I have a stomachache.	**Tenho uma dor de estômago.** <u>teh</u>·nyoo oonga daur deh ee·<u>stau</u>·muh·goo

Finding a Doctor

Can you recommend a *doctor/dentist*?	**Pode recomendar um *médico/ dentista*?** pawd reh·koo·mehn·<u>dahr</u> oong *meh·dee·koo/dehn·<u>teeh</u>·stuh*
Could the doctor come to see me here?	**O médico podia vir cá ver-me [aqui me ver]?** oo <u>meh</u>·dee·koo poo·<u>thee</u>·uh veer kah <u>vehr</u>·meh [uh·<u>kee</u> meh vehr]
I need an English-speaking doctor.	**Preciso de um médico que fale inglês.** preh·<u>see</u>·zoo deh oong <u>meh</u>·dee·koo keh <u>fah</u>·leh eeng·<u>lehz</u>
What are the office hours?	**A que horas é que há consulta?** uh kee <u>aw</u>·ruhz eh keh ah kaun·<u>sool</u>·tuh
I'd like to make an appointment…	**Queria marcar uma consulta…** keh·<u>ree</u>·uh muhr·<u>kahr</u> <u>oo</u>·muh kaun·<u>sool</u>·tuh…
– for today	– **para hoje** <u>puh</u>·ruh auyzseh
– for tomorrow	– **amanhã** <u>puh</u>·ruh uh·muh·<u>nyuh</u>
– as soon as possible	– **o mais cedo possível** oo meyez <u>seh</u>·thoo poo·<u>see</u>·vel
It's urgent.	**É urgente.** eh oor·<u>zsehnt</u>

I'm…	**Estou…** ee·<u>stawoo</u>…
– bleeding	**– a sangrar [sangrando]** uh suhn·<u>grahr</u> [suhn·<u>gruhn</u>·doo]
– constipated	**– constipado** ♂**/constipada** ♀ kaun·stee·<u>pah</u>·thoo ♂/kaun·stee·<u>pah</u>·thuh ♀
– dizzy	**– com a cabeça a roda** kaum uh kuh·<u>beh</u>·suh ah <u>raw</u>·thuh
I'm nauseous.	**Estou enjoado** ♂**/enjoada** ♀. ee·<u>stawoo</u> eng·zsoo·<u>ah</u>·thoo ♂/eng·zsoo·<u>ah</u>·thuh ♀
I'm vomiting.	**Estou a vomitar.** ee·<u>stawoo</u> uh voo·mee·<u>tahr</u>
It hurts here.	**Dói-me aqui.** <u>doy</u>·meh uh·<u>kee</u>
I have…	**Tenho…** <u>teh</u>·nyoo…
– an allergic reaction	**– uma reação alérgica** <u>oo</u>·muh rree·ah·<u>sohm</u> uh·<u>lehr</u>·gee·kuh
– chest pain	**– dor de peito** daur deh <u>pay</u>·too
– an earache	**– dor de ouvidos** daur deh aw·<u>vee</u>·thooz
– a fever	**– uma febre** <u>oo</u>·muh <u>feh</u>·breh
– pain	**– dor** daur
– a rash	**– uma erupção cutânea** <u>oo</u>·muh eer·oop·<u>sohm</u> koo·<u>tuh</u>·nee·uh
– a sprain	**– uma distensão muscular** <u>oo</u>·muh dees·tehn·<u>sohm</u> <u>moos</u>·koo·lahr
– some swelling	**– algum inchaço** <u>ahl</u>·goong een·<u>shah</u>·soo
– a stomachache	**– dor de estômago** daur deh ee·<u>stau</u>·muh·goo
I have sunstroke.	**Apanhei uma insolação.** uh·puh·<u>nyay</u> <u>oo</u>·muh een·soo·luh·<u>sohm</u>
I've been sick [ill] for…days.	**Há…dias que me sinto doente.** ah… <u>dee</u>·uhz keh meh <u>seen</u>·too doo·<u>ehnt</u>

▶For numbers, see page 177.

Health Conditions

I'm...	**Sou...** sawoo...
– anemic	– **anêmico** ♂/**anêmica** ♀ uh-neh-mee-koo ♂/ uh-neh-mee-kuh ♀
– diabetic	– **diabético** ♂/**diabética** ♀ dee-uh-beh-tee-koo ♂/dee-uh-beh-tee-kuh ♀
– asthmatic	– **asmático** ♂/**asmática** ♀ uhz-mah-tee-koo ♂/ uhz-mah-tee-kuh ♀
I'm allergic to *antibiotics/penicillin*.	**Sou alérgico** ♂/**alérgica** ♀ **a** *antibiótica/ penicilina.* sawoo uh-lehr-gee-koo ♂/ uh-lehr-gee-kuh ♀ uh *uhn-tee-bee-aw-tee-kuh/ peh-neh-seh-lee-nuh*

▶ For food items, see page 89.

I have *arthritis/(high/ low) blood pressure.*	**Tenho** *artrite/a pressão arterial (alta/baixa).* teh-nyoo uh-treet/uh preh-sohm uhr-teh-ree-ahl (ahl-tuh/beye-shuh)
I have a heart condition.	**Tenho um problema de coração.** teh-nyoo oong proo-bleh-muh deh koo-ruh-sohm
I'm on...	**Estou em...** ee-stawoo eng...

You May Hear...

Qual é o problema? kwahl eh oo proo-bleh-muh	What's the problem?
Onde é que lhe dói? aund eh keh lyeh doy	Where does it hurt?
Dói-lhe aqui? doy-lyeh uh-kee	Does it hurt here?
Toma medicamentos? taw-muh meh-dee-kuh-mehn-tooz	Are you on medication?
És alérgico ♂/**alérgica** ♀ **a algo?** ehz uh-lehr-zsee-koo ♂/uh-lehr-zsee-kuh ♀ uh ahl-goo	Are you allergic to anything?
Abra a boca. ah-bruh uh bau-kuh	Open your mouth.

Respire fundo. rehs·<u>pee</u>·reh <u>foon</u>·doo

Breathe deeply.

Quero que vá para o hospital. <u>keh</u>·roo keh vah <u>puh</u>·ruh oo aws·pee·<u>tahl</u>

I want you to go to the hospital.

Hospital

Please notify my family.	**Por favor informe a minha família.** poor fuh·<u>vaur</u> eeng·<u>fawr</u>·meh uh <u>mee</u>·nyuh fuh·<u>mee</u>·lyuh
I'm in pain.	**Estou com dores.** ee·<u>stawoo</u> kaun <u>daur</u>·ehz
I need a *doctor/nurse*.	**Necessito *um médico/uma enfermeira*.** neh·seh·<u>see</u>·too *oong <u>meh</u>·dee·koo/<u>oo</u>·muh een·fehr·<u>may</u>·ruh*
When are visiting hours?	**Quais são as horas de visitas?** kweyez sohm uhz <u>aw</u>·ruhz deh vee·<u>zee</u>·tuhz
I'm visiting…	**Estou a visitar…** ee·<u>stawoo</u> uh vee·see·<u>tahr</u>…

Dentist

I've broken a tooth/lost a filling.	**Parti um dente./Perdi um chumbo.** pehr·thee oong dehnt/pehr·<u>thee</u> oong <u>shoom</u>·boo
I have a toothache.	**Tenho dore de dentes.** <u>teh</u>·nyoo daur deh dehntz
Can you fix this denture?	**Pode consertar esta dentadura?** pawd kaun·sehr·<u>tahr</u> <u>eh</u>·stuh dehn·tuh·<u>doo</u>·ruh

Gynecologist

I have *menstrual cramps/a vaginal infection*.	**Tenho *dores períodos menstruais/uma infecção na vagina*.** <u>teh</u>·nyoo *daurz pehr·ree·<u>oo</u>·thooz mehn·stroo·<u>eyez</u>/<u>oo</u>·muh eeng·feh·<u>sohm</u> nuh vuh·<u>zsee</u>·nuh*
I missed my period.	**Faltou-me o meu período.** fahl·<u>tawoo</u>·meh oo meeoo peh·ree·<u>oo</u>·thoo

I'm on the pill.	**Estou a tomar [tomando] a pílula.** ee·<u>stawoo</u> uh too·<u>mar</u> [too·<u>muhn</u>·doo] uh <u>pee</u>·loo·luh
I'm (not) pregnant.	**(Não) Estou grávida.** (nohm) ee·<u>stawoo</u> <u>grah</u>·vee·thuh
I haven't had my period for…months.	**Já não tenho o meu período á…meses.** zsah nohm <u>teh</u>·nyoo oo mehoo peh·ree·<u>oo</u>·thoo ah…<u>meh</u>·zehz

Optician

I've lost…	**Perdi…** pehr·<u>thee</u>…
– one of my contact lenses	– **uma das minhas lentes de contacto** <u>oo</u>·muh duhz <u>mee</u>·nyuhz <u>lehn</u>·tehz deh kaun·<u>tahk</u>·too
– my glasses	– **os meus óculos** ooz mehooz <u>aw</u>·koo·looz
– a lens	– **uma lente** <u>oo</u>·muh lehnt

Payment and Insurance

How much?	**Quanto é?** <u>kwuhn</u>·too eh
Can I pay by credit card?	**Posso pagar com cartão de crédito?** <u>paw</u>·soo puh·<u>gahr</u> kaum oo kuhr·<u>tohm</u> deh <u>kreh</u>·dee·too
I have insurance.	**Tenho seguro.** <u>teh</u>·nyoo seh·<u>goo</u>·roo
Can you give me a receipt for my health insurance?	**Pode dar-me [Podia me dar] um recibo para o meu seguro de saúde?** pawd <u>dar</u>·meh [poo·<u>dee</u>·uh meh dar] oong reh·<u>see</u>·boo <u>puh</u>·ruh oo mehoo seh·<u>goo</u>·roo deh suh·<u>oo</u>·theh

Pharmacy [Chemist]

Essential

Where's the pharmacy [chemist]?	**Onde fica a farmácia?** aund <u>fee</u>·kuh uh fuhr·<u>mah</u>·see·uh
What time does the pharmacy *open/ close*?	**A que horas é que a farmácia *abre/fecha*?** uh keh <u>aw</u>·ruhz eh keh uh fuhr·<u>mah</u>·see·uh *<u>ah</u>·breh/<u>feh</u>·shuh*
What would you recommend for...?	**O que é que me recomenda para...?** oo keh eh keh meh reh·koo·<u>mehn</u>·duh <u>puh</u>·ruh...
How much should I take?	**Quanto é que devo tomar?** <u>kwuhn</u>·too eh keh <u>deh</u>·voo too·<u>mahr</u>
Can you fill [make up] this prescription for me?	**Pode aviar-me esta receita?** pawd uh·vee·<u>ahr</u>·meh <u>eh</u>·stuh reh·<u>say</u>·tuh
I'm allergic to...	**Sou alérgico ♂/alérgica ♀ a...** sawoo uh·<u>lehr</u>·zsee·koo ♂/uh·<u>lehr</u>·zsee·kuh ♀ ah...

Pharmacies are easily recognized by their sign: a green or red cross, usually lit up. You'll find the address of all-night pharmacies (**farmácia de cerviço**) displayed in all pharmacy windows.

In Portugal, pharmacies sell pharmaceutical products, and sometimes a small supply of cosmetics as well—also available in a **perfumaria**. Household and toilet articles can be bought from a **drogaria**. In the pharmacies in Brazil, you can normally find medicines, perfume, cosmetics and household articles. Travelers who use prescription medicine should bring enough with them to cover their stay.

Dosage Instructions

How much should I take?	**Quanto é que devo tomar?** <u>kwuhn</u>·too eh keh <u>deh</u>·voo too·<u>mahr</u>
How often should I take it?	**Quantas vezes é que devo tomar?** <u>kwuhn</u>·tuhz <u>veh</u>·zehz eh keh <u>deh</u>·voo too·<u>mahr</u>
Is it suitable for children?	**É próprio para crianças?** eh <u>praw</u>·pree·oo <u>puh</u>·ruh kree·<u>uhn</u>·suhs
I'm taking…	**Estou a tomar…** ee·<u>stawoo</u> uh too·<u>mahr</u>…
Are there side effects?	**Há efeitos colaterais?** ah ee·<u>fay</u>·tooz kaw·<u>luh</u>·tehr·eyez

You May See…

UMA VEZ/ TRES VEZES POR DIA	*once/three times* a day
COMPRIMIDO(S)	tablet(s)
GOTA	drop
COLHERE(S) DE CHÁ	teaspoon(s)
ANTES DAS/ DEPOIS DAS/ COM AS REFEIÇÕES	*before/after/with* meals
NUM ESTÔMAGO VAZIO	on an empty stomach
POSSA CAUSAR SONOLÊNCIA	may cause drowsniness
PARA USO EXTERNO	for external use only

Health Problems

I'd like some medicine for…	**Queria medicina para…** keh·<u>ree</u>·uh meh·deh·<u>see</u>·nuh <u>puh</u>·ruh…
– a cold	**– uma constipação [um resfriado]** <u>oo</u>·muh kaun·stee·puh·<u>sohm</u> [oong rehz·free·<u>ah</u>·do]
– a cough	**– uma tosse** <u>oo</u>·muh <u>taw</u>·seh

Health

– diarrhea	– **a diarreia** uh dee·uh·<u>rray</u>·uh
– insect bites	– **as picadas de insecto** uhz pee·<u>kah</u>·duhz deh eeng·<u>sehk</u>·too
– motion [travel] sickness	– **o enjoo** oo ehn·<u>zsau</u>·oo
– a sore throat	– **a dor de garganta** uh daur deh guhr·<u>guhn</u>·tuh
– sunburn	– **uma queimadura de sol** <u>oo</u>·muh kay·muh·<u>doo</u>·ruh deh sawl
– an upset stomach	– **uma indisposição gástrica** <u>oo</u>·muh een·dees·poo·zee·<u>sohm</u> <u>gahz</u>·tree·kuh

Basic Needs

I'd like…   **Queria…** keh·<u>ree</u>·uh…

– acetaminophen [paracetamol]	– **acetaminofen** uh·seht·uh·meen·aw·<u>feng</u> [puh·ruh·<u>seh</u>·tuh·mawl]
– antiseptic cream	– **uma pomada antiséptica** oo·muh poo·<u>mah</u>·duh uhn·tee·<u>sehp</u>·tee·kuh
– aspirin	– **uma aspirina** <u>oo</u>·muh uhz·pee·<u>ree</u>·nuh
– bandages	– **umas ligaduras [ataduras]** <u>oo</u>·muhz lee·guh·<u>doo</u>·ruhz [uh·tuh·<u>doo</u>·ruhz]
– a comb	– **um pente** oong pehnt
– condoms	– **uns preservativos** oongz preh·sehr·vuh·<u>tee</u>·vooz
– contact lens solution	– **um líquido de lente de contato** oong <u>lee</u>·kee·thoo deh lehnt deh kaun·<u>tah</u>·too
– deodorant	– **um desodorizante** oong dehz·aw·doo·ree·<u>zuhnt</u>
– a hairbrush	– **uma escova de cabelo** <u>oo</u>·muh ees·<u>kau</u>·vuh deh kuh·<u>beh</u>·loo

171

I'd like...	**Queria...** keh·<u>ree</u>·uh...
– hair spray	– **laca [laquê] para o cabelo** <u>lah</u>·kuh [<u>lah</u>·keh] puh·ruh oo kuh·<u>beh</u>·loo
– ibuprofen	– **ibuprofen** ee·boo·<u>praw</u>·feng
– insect repellent	– **um repelente para insectos** oong reh·peh·<u>lehnt</u> puh·ruh een·<u>sehk</u>·tooz
– a nail file	– **uma lima** <u>oo</u>·muh <u>lee</u>·muh
– (disposable) razor	– **uma gilete (disponível)** <u>oo</u>·muh zsee·<u>leht</u> (dehz·poo·<u>nee</u>·vehl)
– razor blades	– **umas lâminas de barbear** <u>oo</u>·muhz <u>luh</u>·mee·nuhz deh buhr·bee·<u>ahr</u>
– sanitary napkins [pads]	– **uns pensos [absorventes] higiénicos** oongz <u>pehn</u>·sooz [uhb·sawr·<u>vehntz</u>] ee·<u>zseh</u>·nee·kooz
– shampoo/ conditioner	– **um shampoo [xampu]/amaciador [condicionador] para cabelo** oong shuhm·<u>poo</u> [shuhm·<u>poo</u>] uh·muh·see·uh·<u>daur</u> [kaun·dee·see·oo·nuh·<u>daur</u>] puh·ruh kuh·<u>beh</u>·lo
– soap	– **um sabonete** oong suh·boo·<u>neht</u>
– sunscreen	– **um protector solar** oong praw·teh·<u>taur</u> soo·<u>lahr</u>
– tampons	– **uns tampões higiénicos** oongz tuhm·<u>poingz</u> ee·<u>zseh</u>·nee·kooz
– tissues	– **uns lenços de papel** oongz <u>lehn</u>·sooz deh puh·<u>pehl</u>
– toilet paper	– **papel higiénico** puh·<u>pehl</u> ee·<u>zseh</u>·nee·koo
– toothpaste	– **uma pasta de dentes** oo·muh <u>pah</u>·stuh deh dehntz

▶ For baby products, see page 156.

Grammar

In Portuguese, there are three ways to say "you" (taking different verb forms):

In Portugal, **tu** is used when talking to a relative your age or younger, a close friend, or a child (and between young people); in Brazil, **tu** is hardly ever used. **Tu** refers to just one person at a time, and it takes the second person singular of the verb.

In Portugal, **você(s)** is used in more formal situations, between people who don't know each other well and as a sign of respect for family members, anyone older than you, more educated than you, or in business. In most parts of Brazil **você** is predominantly used when talking to anyone, regardless of age or class, even in cases when **tu** would be used in Portugal. **Você(s)** takes either the second person singular or the second person plural of the verb depending on wether you're referring to one person (você) or more than one person (vocês).

The most formal way of saying "you" is **o(s) senhor(es)** to a man (men) and **a(s) senhora(s)** to a woman (women). This is the case in both Portugal and Brazil. **O(s) senhor(es)** and **a(s) senhora(s)** take either the third person singular of the verb or the third person plural depending on whether you're referring to one person (o senhor/a senhora) or more than one person (os senhores/as senhoras).

Regular Verbs

Here are three of the main categories of regular verbs in the present tense:

	-ar	-er	-ir
	falar (to speak)	**comer** (to eat)	**cobrir** (to cover)
eu	falo	como	cubro
tu	falas	comes	cobres
el/ela	fala	come	cobre
nós	falamos	comemos	cobrimos
vós	falais	coméis	cobris
eles/elas	falam	comem	cobrem

Irregular Verbs

In Portuguese there are two main verbs meaning "to be", both of which are irregular.

Ser indicates a permanent state:
Sou inglês.	I'm English.
É portuguesa.	She is Portuguese.

Estar indicates movement or a temporary state:
Está doente.	He is ill.
Estou a passear [passeando].	I am walking.

Nouns and Articles

Nouns in Portuguese are either masculine or feminine. Masculine nouns usually end in **-o** and feminine nouns in **-a**. Normally nouns that end in a vowel become plural by adding an **-s**.

Articles must agree with the noun to which they refer in gender and number.

Indefinite: **um carro** (a train); **uns carros**
(some trains); **uma casa** (a house); **umas** casas (some houses)

Definte: **o carro** (the train); **os carros**
(some trains); **a casa** (the house); **as casas** (the houses)

Word Order

In Portuguese, the conjugated verb comes after the subject.

Maria falo inglês. Maria speaks English.

To ask a question, reverse the order of the subject and verb, change your intonation or use key question words such as **quando** (when).

Quando abre o museu? When does the museum open?

Literally translates to: "When opens the museum?"

É portuguesa? Is she Portuguese?

Literally: She is Portuguese. This is a statement that becomes a question by raising the pitch of the last syllable of the sentence.

Negation

To form a negative sentence, add **não** (not) before the verb.

Fumamos. We smoke.

Não fumamos. We don't smoke.

Imperatives

Imperative sentences, commands, are formed by adding the appropriate ending to the stem of the verb.

Fale! Speak!

Abra a janela, por favor. Open the window, please.

Comparative and Superlative

The comparative is usually formed by adding **mais** (more) or **menos** (less) before the adjective or noun. The superlative is formed by adding the appropriate definite article (**o/os**, **a/as**) and **mais** (the most) or **menos** (the least).

grande	mais grande	o mais grande
big	bigger	biggest
caro	menos caro	o menos caro
expensive	less expensive	least expensive

Possessive Pronouns

Pronouns serve as substitutes for specific nouns and must agree with the noun in gender and number.

meu ♂/**minha** ♀	mine
teu ♂/**tua** ♀	yours
seu ♂/**sua** ♀	yours (*formal*)
nossa	ours
vossa	yours (*plural*)

Example: **Esse assento é o meu.** That seat is mine.

Adjectives

Adjectives describe nouns and must agree with the noun in gender and number. In Portuguese, adjectives usually come after the noun. Masculine adjectives usually end in **-o**, feminine adjectives in **-a**. If the masculine form ends in **-e** (**intellegente**) or with a consonant (**fácil**), the feminine form is generally the same.

O filho/A filha é amável. Your son/daughter is nice.

O mar/A flor azul. The blue ocean/flower.

Adverbs and Adverbial Expressions

Adverbs are used to describe verbs. Some adverbs are formed by adding **-mente** to the singular feminine form of the adjective.

Example: **sincera + mente = sinceramente**

The following are some common adverbial time expressions:

agora	now
ainda não	not yet
ainda	still
nunca	never
sempre	always

Numbers

Essential	
0	**zero** <u>zeh</u>·roo
1	**um** ♂/**uma** ♀ oong ♂/<u>oo</u>·muh ♀
2	**dois** ♂/**duas** ♀ doyz ♂/<u>thoo</u>·uhz ♀
3	**três** trehz
4	**quatro** <u>kwah</u>·troo
5	**cinco** <u>seeng</u>·koo
6	**seis** sayz
7	**sete** seht
8	**oito** <u>oy</u>·too
9	**nove** nawv
10	**dez** dehz
11	**onze** aunz
12	**doze** dauz
13	**treze** trehz
14	**catorze** kuh·<u>taurz</u>
15	**quinze** keengz
16	**dezasseis [dezesseis]** dehz·eh·<u>sayz</u>

17	**dezassete [dezessete]** dehz·eh·<u>seht</u>	
18	**dezoito** dehz·<u>oy</u>·too	
19	**dezanove [dezenove]** deh·zuh·<u>nawv</u>	
20	**vinte** veent	
21	**vinte e um** ♂ **/uma** ♀ veent ee oong ♂ / <u>oo</u>·muh ♀	
22	**vinte e dois** ♂ **/duas** ♀ veent ee doyz ♂ / <u>thoo</u>·uhz ♀	
30	**trinta** <u>treeng</u>·tuh	
31	**trinta e um** ♂ **/uma** ♀ <u>treeng</u>·tuh ee oong ♂ / <u>oo</u>·muh ♀	
40	**quarenta** kwuh·<u>rehn</u>·tuh	
50	**cinquenta** seeng·<u>kwehn</u>·tuh	
60	**sessenta** seh·<u>sehn</u>·tuh	
70	**setenta** seh·<u>tehn</u>·tuh	
80	**oitenta** oy·<u>tehn</u>·tuh	
90	**noventa** noo·<u>vehn</u>·tuh	
100	**cem** sehn	
101	**cento e um** ♂ **/uma** ♀ <u>sehn</u>·too ee oong ♂ / <u>oo</u>·muh ♀	
200	**duzentos** ♂ **/duzentas** ♀ doo·<u>zehn</u>·tooz ♂ / doo·<u>zehn</u>·tuhz ♀	
500	**quinhentos** ♂ **/quinhentas** ♀ kee·<u>nyehn</u>·tooz ♂ /kee·<u>nyehn</u>·tuhz ♀	
1,000	**mil** meel	
10,000	**dez mil** dehz meel	
1,000,000	**um milhão** oong mee·<u>lyohm</u>	

Ordinal Numbers

first	**o primeiro** ♂/**a primeira** ♀ oo pree·<u>may</u>·roo ♂/ uh pree·<u>may</u>·ruh ♀
second	**o segundo** ♂/**a segunda** ♀ oo seh·<u>goon</u>·doo ♂/uh seh·<u>goon</u>·duh ♀
third	**o terceiro** ♂/**a terceira** ♀ oo tehr·<u>say</u>·roo ♂/ uh tehr·<u>say</u>·ruh ♀
fourth	**o quarto** ♂/**a quarta** ♀ oo <u>kwahr</u>·too ♂/ uh <u>kwahr</u>·tuh ♀
fifth	**o quinto** ♂/**a quinta** ♀ oo <u>keen</u>·too ♂/uh <u>keen</u>·tuh ♀
once	**uma vez** <u>oo</u>·muh vehz
twice	**duas vezes** <u>thoo</u>·uhz <u>veh</u>·zehz
three times	**três vezes** trehz <u>veh</u>·zehz

Portuguese uses a comma for a decimal point and a period [full stop] or space for thousands—e.g., 4,95; 4.575.000 or 4 575 000.

Essential

What time is it?	**As horas, por favor?** uhz <u>aw</u>·ruhz poor fuh·<u>vaur</u>
It's noon [mid-day].	**É meio-dia.** eh <u>may</u>·oo dee·uh
At midnight.	**Á meia-noite.** ah <u>may</u>·uh noyt
From nine o'clock to five o'clock.	**Das nove às cinco horas.** duhz nawv ahz <u>seeng</u>·koo <u>aw</u>·ruhz
Twenty [after] past four.	**Quatro e vinte.** <u>kwah</u>·troo ee veent
A quarter to nine.	**Um quarto para as nove.** oong <u>kwahr</u>·too <u>puh</u>·ruh uhz nawv
5:30 *a.m./p.m.*	**Cinco e meia *de manhã/da tarde.*** <u>seeng</u>·koo ee <u>may</u>·uh *deh muh·<u>nyuh</u>/duh tahrd*

In Portugal, digital time is on the 24 hour clock, but time is not referred to in that way. The Portuguese would not say it's "13:00," in speech but rather they would express the the hour along with the time of day, i.e. "one in the afternoon" (**uma hora da tarde**).

Days

Essential

Monday	**segunda-feira** seh·<u>goon</u>·duh <u>fay</u>·ruh
Tuesday	**terça-feira** <u>tehr</u>·suh <u>fay</u>·ruh
Wednesday	**quarta-feira** <u>kwahr</u>·tuh <u>fay</u>·ruh
Thursday	**quinta-feira** <u>keen</u>·tuh <u>fay</u>·ruh
Friday	**sexta-feira** <u>say</u>·stuh <u>fay</u>·ruh
Saturday	**sábado** <u>sah</u>·buh·thoo
Sunday	**domingo** doo·<u>meeng</u>·goo

Dates

yesterday	**ontem** <u>awn</u>·teng
today	**hoje** auzseh
tomorrow	**amanhã** uh·muh·<u>nuh</u>
today	**o dia** oo <u>dee</u>·uh
week	**a semana** uh seh·<u>muh</u>·nuh
month	**o mês** oo mehz
year	**o ano** oo <u>uh</u>·noo

 Portuguese calendars go from Monday to Sunday. When giving dates, the Portuguese give the day first, then the month, then the year (e.g., 1 May 2009 or 1/5/2009).

181

Months

January	**Janeiro** zher·nay·roo
February	**Fevereiro** feh·vray·roo
March	**Março** mahr·soo
April	**Abril** uh·breel
May	**Maio** meye·oo
June	**Junho** zsoo·nyoo
July	**Julho** zsoo·lyoo
August	**Agosto** uh·gaus·too
September	**Setembro** seh·tehm·broo
October	**Outubro** aw·too·broo
November	**Novembro** noo·vehm·broo
December	**Dezembro** deh·zehm·broo

Seasons

the spring	**a primavera** uh pree·muh·veh·ruh
the summer	**o verão** oo vrohm
the fall [autumn]	**o outono** oo aw·too·noo
the winter	**o inverno** oo eeng·verr·noo

Holidays

The dates of **Carnaval** are based on the dates of Lent and Easter, and therefore change every year. **Carnaval** starts on the Saturday before Ash Wednesday and lasts until Ash Wednesday.

Some major national holidays in Portugal and Brazil are:

January 1	New Year's Day	Port.	Braz.
January 6	Epiphany	Port.	Braz.
April 11	Tiradentes Day		Braz.
April 25	Freedom Day	Port.	
May 1	May Day	Port.	Braz.
June 10	Camões Day	Port.	
August 15	Assumption Day	Port.	Braz.
September 7	Independence Day		Braz.
October 1	Our Lady of Aparecida Day	Port.	Braz.
October 5	Republic Day	Port.	
November 1	All Saints' Day	Port.	Braz.
November 15	Proclamation Day		Braz.
December 1	Restoration Day	Port.	
December 8	Immaculate Conception Day	Port.	Braz.
December 25	Christmas Day	Port.	Braz.

i

On January 6th, in celebration of the Epiphany, it is customary for the Portuguese to eat a breadlike cake in the shape of a king's crown, topped with dried fruit.

In observance of Our Lady of Aparecida Day, on October 1st, thousands of Portuguese pay tribute to our Lady of Fatima to celebrate the "Miracle of the Sun" of 1917. They express their faith by walking (or even crawling to show their devotion) from their hometowns to Our Lady of Fatima Church in Fatima, a town in the district of Santarém in central Portugal (187 km south of Porto and 123 km north of Lisbon).

Conversion Tables

Mileage

1 km – 0.62 mi	20 km – 12.4 mi
5 km – 3.10 mi	50 km – 31.0 mi
10 km – 6.20 mi	100 km – 61.0 mi

Measurement

1 gram	**grama**	= 1000 milligrams	= 0.035 oz.
1 kilogram (kg)	**quilo**	= 1000 grams	= 2.2 lb
1 liter (l)	**litro**	= 1000 milliliters	= 1.06 U.S./0.88 Brit. quarts
1 centimeter (cm)	**centímetro**	= 10 millimeters	= 0.4 inch
1 meter (m)	**metro**	= 100 centimeters	= 39.37 inches/3.28 feet
1 kilometer (km)	**quilómetro**	= 1000 meters	= 0.62 mile

Temperature

-40° C – -40° F	5° C – 41° F
-30° C – -22° F	10° C – 50° F
-20° C – -4° F	15° C – 59° F
-10° C – 14° F	20° C – 68° F
-5° C – 23° F	25° C – 77° F
-1° C – 30° F	30° C – 86° F
0° C – 32° F	35° C – 95° F

Oven Temperature

100° C – 212° F	177° C – 350° F
121° C – 250° F	204° C – 400° F
149° C – 300° F	260° C – 500° F

Useful Websites

www.Portugal.org
official site of Portugal

www.Portugal.com
information on where to go

www.JustPortugal.com
travel information

www.cp.ot
Portuguese railway information

www.Lisbon.usembassy.gov
link to the US embassy

www.flytap.com
Portuguese Airline

www.raileurope.com
Rail Europe

www.brasilemb.org
Brazilian Embassy in Washington, D.C.

www.brasil.gov.br
*Government of Brazil
(Web site in Portuguese)*

www.braziltour.com
*Ministry of Tourism
(Web site in English)*

www.v-brazil.com
tourism information

www.brazilink.org
Brazilian development issues

www.brazilink.org/brazil_travel.asp
Brazil travel

www.brazilcham.com
*Brazilian-American Chamber of
Commerce, Inc.*

English–Portuguese Dictionary

A

a.m. da manhã
abbey a abadia
able capaz
about àcerca de
above acima
abroad no estrangeiro
abscess o abcesso
accept aceitar
access o acesso
accident o acidente
accidentally sem querer
accommodation o alojamento
accompany acompanhar
accountant o contabilista [contador]
activity a actividade
across do outro lado
adaptor o adaptador
address o endereço, a morada
adjoining room o quarto contíguo
admission charge o preço de entrada
adult o adulto
aerobics aeróbica
after depois
afternoon tarde
aftershave a loção para depois da barba [a loção após barba]

after-sun lotion a loção para depois do sol
age a idade
ago há
agree concordar
air conditioning o ar condicionado
air mattress o colchão pneumático [o colchão de ar]
air pump a máquina pneumática [a bomba de ar]
airline a linha aérea
airmail a via aérea
airport o aeroporto
aisle seat o lugar na coxia [o lugar de corredor]
alarm clock o despertador
alcoholic drink a bebida alcoólica
all tudo
allergic alérgico
allergy a alergia
allow permitir
almost quase
alone sózinho
already já
also também
alter modificar
alternate route a rota alternada [o caminho alternativo]
aluminum foil o papel de alumínio
always sempre
ambassador o embaixador
ambulance a ambulância

adj	adjective	adv	adverb	BE	British English
n	noun	v	verb		

American o americano, a americana
anesthetic o anestéstico
and e
announcement anúncio
another outro, outra
answer atender [responder]
antibiotic o antibiótico
antifreeze o anticongelante
antique a antiguidade
antiseptic cream a pomada
  antiséptica
any algum
anyone else mais alguém
anyone alguém
anything alguma coisa
apartment o apartamento
apologize pedir desculpa
apology a desculpa
appointment o apontamento
  [o encontro]
approximately aproximadamente
archery o tiro ao arco
architect o arquitecto, a arquitecta
architecture a arquitectura
area a área
area code o indicativo [código]
around (the corner) ao virar da
  esquina
arrange arranjar
arrivals (airport) as chegadas
arrive chegar
art a arte
art gallery a galeria de arte
artificial sweetener o adoçante
artist o/a artista
ashtray o cinzeiro

ask pedir
asleep adormecido, adormecida
aspirin a aspirina
at least pelo menos
athletics atletismo
attack o ataque
attendant o empregado,
  a empregada
attractive atraente
aunt a tia
Australia a Austrália
Australian (noun) o australiano,
  a australiana
authentic autêntico
authenticity autenticidade
automatic (car) o carro de
  mudanças automáticas
automatic teller machine (ATM)
  o multibanco
avalanche a avalanche
away longe
awful horrível

B

baby o bebé [neném];
  ~sitter baby-sitter [a ama];
  ~wipes os toalhetes de limpeza
  para o bebé [neném]
baby bottle o biberom
  [a mamadeira]
back as costas
bachache a dor de costas
backpack a mochila
bacon toucinho
bad mau, má
bakery a padaria

balcony a varanda
ball a bola
ballet o ballet [o balê]
band (musical) a banda musical
bandage a ligadura [a atadura]
bank o banco
bar o bar
barber o barbeiro
baseball basebol
basement a cave
basin a bacia
basket o cesto
basketball basquetebol
bath o banho
bathe tomar banho
bathroom a casa de banho
  [o banheiro]
battery a pilha; ~ (car, computer)
  a bateria
battle site o campo de batalha
be *v* ser; ~ (temporary state) estar;
  ~ (location) ficar
beach a praia
beard a barba
beautiful bonito, bonita
because porque; ~ of por causa de
bed a cama; ~ and breakfast
  quarto e pequeno-almoço
  [pernoite e café da manhã]
bedding a roupa de cama
bedroom o quarto (de dormir)
bee a abelha
beer a cerveja
before antes de
begin *v* começar
beginner o/a principiante

beginning o começo
beige beige [bege]
belong pertencer
belt o cinto
best melhor
better melhor
between entre
bib a babete [o babador]
bicycle a bicicleta
big grande
bigger o/a maior
bikini o bikini [o biquíni]
binoculars os binóculos
bird o pássaro
bishop o bispo
bite (insect) a picada (de insecto)
bitter azedo
bizarre estranho
black preto
blanket o cobertor
bleach a lixívia [alvejante]
blouse a blusa
blow-dry o secador
blue azul
blueberry o mirtilo
board embarcar
boarding (plane) embarque
boarding pass cartão de embarque
boat o barco
boiled cozido
book *n* o livro
book *v* reservar
book of tickets a caderneta de
  bilhetes
bookstore a livraria

boots as botas
border a fronteira
boring aborrecido
botanical garden o jardim botânico
bottle a garrafa; ~ opener
  o abre-garrafas [o abridor de garrafas]
bowl a malga
box office a bilheteira
boxing o boxe
boy o rapaz
boyfriend o namorado
bra o sutiã
bracelet a pulseira
brake n o travão [o freio]
brass o latão
Brazil o Brasil
Brazilian brasileiro
bread o pão
break v partir [quebrar]
breakdown avariar [quebrar]
break-in o assalto
breakfast o pequeno-almoço
  [o café da manhã]
breathe v respirar
bridge a ponte
briefcase a pasta
briefs as calcinhas
brilliant brilhante
bring v trazer
Britain a Grã-Bretanha
British britânico
brochure o folheto
bronze o bronze
brother o irmão
brown o castanho

brush a escova
bucket (pail) o balde
build v construir
building o edifício
built construído
burger o hambúrguer
burglary o roubo
burnt queimado
bus o autocarro; ~ (long-distance)
  a camioneta; ~ station a estação
  de autocarros; ~ stop a paragem
  [a parada] de autocarro
business class (em) business;
  ~ a trip viagem de negócios
business card o cartão
busy ocupado
but mas
butcher shop o talho [o açougue]
butter a manteiga
button o botão
buy v comprar
bye adeus [adeus]

C

cabin a cabina [o camarote]
cable car o funicular; o teleférico
café o café
cake o bolo
calendar o calendário
call v chamar
camcorder a câmara vídeo
camera a máquina fotográfica;
  ~ case o estojo para a máquina;
  ~ store a loja de artigos fotográficos
camp v acampar

camping campismo [camping];
~ **equipment** o material de campismo [camping]

campsite o parque de campismo [camping]

can n a lata; ~ **opener** o abre-latas [o abridor de latas]

Canadá o Canadá

Canadian canadiano [canadense]

canal o canal

cancel v cancelar

cancer (disease) o cancro [o câncer]

candle a vela

candy os rebuçados [as balas]

canoe a canoa

canoeing fazer canoagem

canyon o desfiladeiro

car o carro; ~ **hire [BE]** aluguer [aluguel] de carros; ~ **park [BE]** o parque de estacionamento;
~ **rental** aluguer [aluguel] de carros

carafe o jarro

card o cartão; **ATM** ~ o cartão multibanco; **credit** ~ o cartão de crédito; **debit** ~ o cartão de débito; **phone** ~ o cartão de chamadas

cards as cartas

carpet o tapete

carry transportar

carry-on levar

carton o pacote

cash o dinheiro

cash v cobrar

casino o casino

castle o castelo

cat o gato [a gata]

catch v (bus) apanhar o autocarro [o ônibus]

cathedral a catedral

cause v causar

cave a caverna

CD o CD

CD-player o leitor de CDs [o tocador de discos compactos]

cell phone o telemóvel

celcius celsius

cemetery o cemitério

cent o cêntimo

certificate o certificado

chair a cadeira

change n (coins) trocado;
~ v (bus) mudar (de autocarro);
~ v (clothes) trocar (de roupa);
~ v (money) trocar dinheiro;
~ v (reservation) mudar a reserva

changing rooms os vestiários

channel (sea) o canal

chapel a capela

charcoal o carvão

charge a tarifa

cheap barato

cheaper mais barato

check (bill) a conta; **put it on the**
~ ponha na conta

check v verificar

checkbook o livro [talão] de cheques

check-in desk o balcão de registo [de registro]

check out v (hotel) pagar a conta

checking account a conta corrente

checkout (supermarket) a caixa

cheers à sua saúde

cheese o queijo

chemical toilet a fossa séptica

chemist a farmácia

chickenpox a varicela

child o menino [a criança]

child's seat a cadeirinha de criança; ~ (in car) a cadeira de criança

chips [BE] as batatas fritas

church aigreja

cigarette o cigarro

cigars os charutos

cinema o cinema

class a classe

clean *adj.* limpo [limpa]

clean *v* limpar

cleaner (person) o empregado da limpeza; ~ (product) o produto de limpeza

cliff a falésia

cling film [BE] o papel aderente

clock o relógio

close (near) perto

close *v* fechar

clothes a roupa; ~ dryer a máquina de secar [o centrifugador]

clothing store a loja de artigos de vestuário

cloudy nublado

clown o palhaço

clubs (golf) os tacos de golfe

coast a costa

coat o casaco [comprido]

cockroach a barata

coffee o café

coin a moeda

cold frio; ~ (illness) a constipação [o resfriado]

colleague o colega

collect *v* vir buscar

college o colégio

color a cor

comb o pente

comedy a comédia

comforter o edredão

commission a comissão

compartment (train) o compartimento

compass o compasso

complain reclamar

complaint a reclamação

computer o computador

conditioner (hair) o amaciador [o condicionador] para o cabelo

condom o preservativo

conductor (orchestra) o maestro

conference a conferência

confirm *v* confirmar

confirmation a confirmação

connect ligar [conectar]

connection (flight) ligação

conscious consciente

constipation a prisão de ventre

consulate o consulado

contact *v* contactar

contact lens as lentes de contacto

contain *v* conter

contagious contagioso

contraceptive o contraceptivo

convenient conveniente

cook o cozinheiro, a cozinheira

cook *v* cozinhar

cool (temperature) fresco
copper o cobre
corkscrew o saca-rolhas
corn o milho
corner a esquina
correct correcto
cost o custo
cot a cama de bebé [nenén], o berço
cotton o algodão
cough n a tosse; ~ v tossir
country (nation) o país
countryside o campo
couple (pair) o par
course (meal) o prato
cousin o primo [a prima]
crash n (car) o desastre [o acidente]
credit card o cartão de crédito;
   ~ number o número do cartão
   de crédito
cross v (road) atravessar
crowded com muita gente
cruise o cruzeiro
crystal o cristal
cup a chávena
cupboard o armário
currency a moeda
currency exchange (office) loja de
   câmbio
customs a alfândega; ~ declaration
   declaração da alfândega
cut n o corte; ~ v cortar
cycling [BE] o ciclismo

D

daily diariamente
damage avariado
damp húmido
dance n a dança; ~ v dançar;
   ~ club o clube de dansa
dangerous perigoso
dark escuro
daughter filha
dawn a madrugada
day o dia
dead morto; ~ (battery)
   descarregada
deaf surdo
debit card (Port) o cartão de débito
deck chair a cadeira de encosto
declare v declarar
decline o declínio
deduct v (money) deduzir
deep profundo
degrees (temperature) os graus
delay o atraso
delete (computer) apagar
delicatessen a charcuteria
delicious delicioso
deliver v entregar
denim a ganga [brim]
dental floss o fio dental
dentist o dentista
deodorant o desodorizante
   [o desodorante]
depart v (train, bus) partida
department store o grande
   armazém [loja de departamentos]
departure (train) a partida

depend depende
deposit *n* o depósito
deposit *v* depositar
destination o destino
detergent detergente
diabetes os diabetes
diabetic o diabético
diamonds os diamantes
diaper a fraldadiarrhea
a diarreia
dictionary o dicionário
diesel o gasóleo [diesel]
difficult difícil
digital digital
dining room a sala de jantar
dinner o jantar
direct *adj* directo
direct *v* indicar
direction a direcção
directory (telephone) a lista
  telefónica
dirty sujo
disabled (person) o/a deficiente
disconnect (computer) desligar
  [desconectar]
discount o desconto
dish (meal) o prato
dishes a louça
dishwashing liquid o detergente
  para a louça
display case a vitrina
disposable (camera) máquina
  descartável
dive *v* mergulhar
divorced divorciado
doctor o médico

dog o cão
doll a boneca
dollar (U.S.) o dólar
domestic (flight) domestico
door a porta
double bed a cama de casal
double room o quarto duplo
down abaixo
downstairs em baixo
downtown o centro da cidade
dozen dúzia
dress *n* **(clothing)** vestido
drink *n* bebida
drinking water água potável
drive *v* conduzir
driver condutor
driver's license a carta de
  condução [carteira de motorista]
drugstore a farmácia
drunk o bêbedo [bêbado]
dry cleaner lavandaria
  [o lavanderia] de limpeza a seco
during durante
dusty poeirento
duty (tax) dever
duty-free goods a mercadoria
  isenta de taxas
duty-free shopping as compras
  duty-free

E

e-ticket e-bilhete electrónico
ear o ouvido
ear drops gotas para os ouvidos
earlier mais cedo
early cedo

earrings os brincos
east leste
easy fácil
eat comer
economy class a classe económica
electricity a electricidade
elevator o elevador
e-mail *n* o email
e-mail *v* enviar emails
e-mail address morada de email
embassy a embaixada
emerald a esmeralda
emergency a emergência;
  ~ emergency exit a saída de
  emergência
empty *adj* vazio [vazia]
enamel (jewelry) esmalte
end *v* terminar
engine o motor
England a Inglaterra
English inglês
enjoy *v* apreciar
enough bastante [suficiente]
enter entrar
entertainment entretenimento
envelope o envelope
equipment (sports) o equipamento
  (desportivo)
erase *v* apagar
error o erro
escalator a escada rolante
essential essencial
EU (European Union) a UE
  (União Europeia)
euro o euro

Europe a Europa

except excepto
excess o excesso
exchange *v* trocar
exchange rate a taxa de câmbio
excursion a excursão
excuse me (apology) desculpe-me;
  (to get attention) desculpe
exhausted *adj* exausto [exausta]
exhibition a exposição
exit a saída
expensive caro
expiration date a data de validade
extremely extremamente
eye o olho

F

face a cara
facial a limpeza de pele
family a família
famous famoso
fan (electric) a ventoinha
  [o ventilador]
far longe
fare o bilhete
farm a quinta
fast depressa
faster mais rápido
fast food as refeições rápidas
fat *n* a gordura; **~** *adj* gordo
fat-free sem gordura
father o pai
faucet a torneira
favorite o preferido
fax *n* o fax
fax *v* enviar fax

fear o medo
feed v alimentar
female a mulher
ferry o ferry
few poucos
fever a febre
field (sports) o campo
fill out v (form) preencher
film (camera) o filme
fine (penalty) a multa
fire n o fogo
fire alarm o alarme de incêndio
fire department [brigade]
os bombeiros
fire escape a saída de incêndio
fire extinguisher o extintor de
incêndio
first o primeiro
first class a primeira classe
first-aid kit o estojo de primeiros
socorros
fit (clothes) servir
fitting room o gabinete de provas
fix v arranjar
flag a bandeira
flash (photography) o flash
flashlight a lanterna
flat (tire) o furo
flight o vôo
flood a inundação
floor (level) o andar
flower a flor
fly (insect) a mosca
fly v voar
food a comida

football [BE] o futebol
forecast a previsão
foreign o estrangeiro; ~ currency
as divisas estrangeiras
forest a floresta
forget v esquecer
fork (utensil) o garfo; ~ (in road)
a bifurcação
form o impresso
formula (baby) a papa
fortunately felizmente
fountain a fonte
free (available) livre;
~ (no charge) grátis
frequently muitas vezes,
frequentemente
fresh fresco
friend o amigo [a amiga]
full cheio
furniture a mobília

G

gallon o galão
game o jogo
garage a garagem [a oficina]
garbage bag o saco para o lixo
garden o jardim
gardener o jardineiro
gasoline a gasolina
gate (airport) a porta
gay club o clube gay
genuine autêntico
get out v sair
gift a oferta
girl a menina

girlfriend a namorada
give *v* dar
give way (on the road) [BE] dar prioridade
glass (drinking) o copo
glass (material) o vidro
glove a luva
go ir
golf o golfe
good bom [boa]; ~ morning bom dia; ~night boa noite
goodbye adeus
gram o grama
grandparent o/a avô
grape a uva
gray o cinzento
green o verde
grocery store a mercearia
ground (camping) o terreno
group o grupo
guarantee a garantia
guide (person) o/a guia
guidebook o guia

H

hair o cabelo; ~brush a escova de cabelo; ~dryer o secador de cabelo; ~gel o gel para o cabelo; ~spray a laca para o cabelo
haircut o corte de cabelo
hairdresser (ladies/men) o cabeleireiro (senhoras/homens)
half metade
hammer o martelo
hand a mão

hand cream o creme para as mãos
hand luggage [BE] a bagagem de mão
handbag [BE] a mala de mão
handicapped o/a deficiente
handicapped accessible acessível a deficientes
hangover a ressaca
happy feliz
hat o chapéu
have *v* ter
head a cabeça
health a saúde
hear *v* ouvir
hearing aid o aparelho auditivo
heater o aquecedor
heating [BE] aquecedor
heavy pesado
height a altura
hello olá
help *n* a ajuda
help *v* ajudar
here aqui
high a altura
high tide a maré alta
highway a auto-estrada
hike (walk) o passeio a pé
hiking fazer longas caminhadas a pé
hill a colina
hire *v* [BE] alugar
hire car [BE] o carro de aluguer [o carro de aluguel]
hitchhike *v* pedir boleia [carona]
hitchhiking à boleia [à carona]
hold *v* (contain) conter

holiday o feriado
holiday [BE] as férias
home a casa
horse o cavalo
horseracing a corrida de cavalos
hospital o
hospital
hostel a pensão
hot (temperature) quente
hot (spicy) picante
hot spring a nascente de água
quente
hot water a água quente; ~ bottle
a botija [a garrafa] de água quente
hotel o hotel
hour a hora
house a casa
household goods os artigos para
a casa
how (question) como
how much (question) quanto
hurt adj o ferido
husband o marido

I

ice o gelo
ice cream o gelado, o sorvete;
~ parlor a gelataria [a sorveteria];
~ cone o cone de gelado [sorvete]
ice hockey o hóquei no gelo
icy adj gelado, gelada
identification a identificação
ill adj o/a doente
illness a doença
in (place) no; ~ (time) em

indoor dentro de casa; ~ pool a
piscina coberta
inexpensive barato
inflammation a inflamação
informal (dress) (o vestido) informal
information a informação
innocent o/a inocente
insect o insecto; ~ bite a picada
de insecto; ~ repellent o repelente
de insectos
inside dentro de
insomnia a insónia
instant coffee o café instantâneo
instant message a mensagem
instantânea
insulin a insulina
insurance o seguro;
~ card a apólice de seguro
interesting interessante
international internacional
Internet cafe o internet café
Internet service o serviço de internet
interpreter o/a intérprete
intersection o cruzamento
introduce v introduzir
invite v convidar
Ireland a Irlanda
Irish irlandês
iron v passar a ferro
island a ilha

J

jam doce
jar o frasco
jeans as calças de ganga

jellyfish a alforreca [a água-viva]

jewelry as jóias

joke a piada

judge o juiz

jumper cables os cabos da bateria

K

key a chave

key card o cartão da porta

kiddie pool a piscina de bebés [nenens]

kilo(gram) o quilo(grama)

kilometer o quilómetro

kiosk o quiosque

kiss beijar

kitchen a cozinha

knee o joelho

L

lace a renda

ladder a escada

lake o lago

large grande

last o último

late (time) tarde; ~ (delayed) atrasado

later mais tarde

launderette [BE] a lavandaria [a lavanderia]

laundromat a lavandaria [a lavanderia]

laundry service o serviço de lavandaria [lavanderia]

lawyer o advogado, a advogada

learn v aprender

leather o cabedal [o couro]

leave v partir

left a esquerda

left-luggage office [BE] o depósito de bagagem

lens a objectiva

less menos

lesson a lição

letter a carta

library a biblioteca

life a vida

lifeboat o barco salva-vidas

lifeguard o banheiro/salva-vidas

life jacket o colete salva-vidas

lift [BE] o elevador

light (shade) claro; ~ (weight) leve

light n a luz

light v ascender

lightbulb a lâmpada (eléctrica)

lighter o isqueiro

lightning o relâmpago

line (waiting) a fila (de espera)

line (subway) a linha

linen o linho

lip o lábio

liquor store a loja de bebidas alcoólicas

liter o litro

little pequeno

live v viver

local regional

lock n a fechadura

locked adj fechado (à chave)

locker o cacifo com fecho

log on v autenticar

log off v sair
long comprido; (time) muito
long-sighted [BE] visto de longe
look v ver
look for procurar
lose v perder
lost adj perdido
lost-and-found os perdidos e achados
lotion a loção
louder mais alto
love (a person) amar; ~ (a thing) gostar de
luggage a bagagem
luggage cart [trolley] o carrinho
luggage locker o cacifo de bagagem
luggage ticket o talão de bagagem
lumpy (mattress) aos altos e baixos
lunch o almoço
lung o pulmão

M

magazine a revista
magnificent magnífico
mail o correio
mailbox a caixa do correio
main course o prato principal
make up a prescription [BE] receitar
male o homem
man o homem
manager o/a gerente
manicure a manicure
manual (gears) (a caixa de velocidades) manual map o mapa
market o mercado

married casado
mass (church service) a missa
massage a massagem
matches (fire) os fósforos
material o material
mattress o colchão
maybe talvez
meal a refeição
mean v significar
measure v medir
measurement o tamanho
meat a carne
medicine o remédio
medium (size) médio; ~ (cooked) meio-passado
meet v encontrar(-se)
mend v consertar
menu o menu
message a mensagem
metal o metal
meter (taxi) o taxímetro
meter (parking) o parquímetro
microwave (oven) o microondas
midday [BE] o meio-dia
migraine a enxaqueca
mileage a quilometragem
minibar o mini-bar [o frigobar]
minute o minuto
mirror o espelho
miss v perder
missing em falta
mistake o engano
misunderstanding o mal-entendido
mobile phone [BE] o telemóvel
mobile home a casa ambulante

modern moderno
money o dinheiro
monument o monumento
moped a lambreta
more mais
mosquito o mosquito
mother a mãe
motion sickness o enjoo
motor o motor
motorbike a motocicleta
motorboat o barco a motor
motorway [BE] a auto-estrada
mountain a montanha; ~ bike
  a bicicleta de montanha
moustache o bigode
mouth a boca
move v mudar(-se)
movie o filme
movie theater o cinema
much muito
mug (drinking) a caneca
mugging o assalto
mumps a papeira [a caxumba]
museum o museu
music a música

N

nail (body) a unha; ~polish o
  verniz [o esmalte] de unhas
name o nome
napkin o guardanapo
nappy [BE] a fralda
narrow estreito
national nacional
nationality a nacionalidade

nature preserve a reserva natural
nausea a náusea
near perto
nearest mais próximo
necessary necessário
neck (body) o pescoço
neck (clothing) a gola
necklace o colar
needle a agulha
neighbor o vizinho
nephew o sobrinho
never nunca
new novo
newspaper o jornal
newsstand [newsagent]
  o quiosque [a banca] de jornais
next próximo
next to ao lado de
niece a sobrinha
night a noite
nightclub o nightclub
no não
no one ninguém
noisy barulhento
non-alcoholic não-alcoólica
non-smoking (adj.) não-fumadores
  [não-fumantes]
none nenhum
normal normal
north o norte
note a nota
note [BE] a nota
notebook o caderno
nothing nada
now agora

number (telephone) o número de telefone

number plate (car) [BE] a placa de matrícula

nurse o enfermeiro, a enfermeira

O

observatory o observatório

occupied ocupado

off-licence [BE] a loja de vinhos

office o escritório

often muitas vezes

oil o óleo

okay O.K.

old o velho

old-fashioned antigo

one um, uma

one-way ticket o bilhete de ida

open v abrir

open adj aberto

opening hours as horas de funcionamento

opera a ópera

operation a operação

opposite o oposto

optician o oculista

orange (fruit) a laranja; **(color)** cor-de-laranja

orchestra a orquestra

order v encomendar

outdoor ao ar livre; **~ pool** a piscina ao ar livre

outside fora de

over sobre

overdone adj cozido demais

overnight só uma noite

P

p.m. da tarde/da noite

pacifier a chupeta

pack v fazer as malas

package o embrulho [o pacote]

paddling pool [BE] a piscina de bebés [nenens]

padlock o cadeado [o aloquete]

pain a dor

paint v pintar

painter o pintor, a pintora

painting o quadro

pajamas o pijama

palace o palácio

pants as calças

pantyhose os collants

paper o papel

paper napkin o guardanapo de papel

park o parque

park v estacionar

parking o estacionamento; **~ lot** o parque de estacionamento; **~ meter** o parquímetro; **~ space** o lugar de estacionamento

partner o companheiro

part a peça

party a festa

pass n o passe

pass v passar

passenger o passageiro, a passageira

passport o passaporte

pastry shop a pastelaria [a confeitaria]

patch v remendar

path o caminho

pay v pagar

201

pay phone o telefone público

peak (mountain) o pico

pearl a pérola

pedestrian crossing a passadeira [a passagem de pedestres]

pedicure a pedicure

pen a caneta

pencil o lápis

penicillin a penicilina

per por: ~ day por dia; ~ hour por hora; ~ night por noite; ~ week por semana

performance a sessão

perfume o perfume

perhaps talvez

period período

permit a permissão; ~ v permitir

petrol [BE] a gasolina; ~ station [BE] a bomba de gasolina

pharmacy a farmácia

phone o telefone; ~ call o telefonema; ~ card o credifone [o cartão telefônico]

photo a fotografia

photocopier a fotocopiadora

photographer o fotógrafo

photography a fotografia

pick up v ir buscar; (collect) levantar

picnic o piquenique; ~ area a área para piqueniques

piece a peça

Pill a pílula

pillow a almofada

personal identification number (PIN) o PIN

pink cor-de-rosa

piste [BE] a pista

piste map [BE] o mapa de pistas

pizzeria a pizzaria

place o lugar

place (a bet) apostar

plane o avião

plant a planta

plastic wrap o papel aderente

plate o prato

platform [BE] a linha [plataforma]

platinum a platina

play v jogar; (instrument) tocar

please se faz favor [por favor]

plug (electric) a ficha [a tomada] (eléctrica)

plunger o desentupidor

pocket o bolso

poison o veneno

police a polícia; ~ report o documento da polícia; ~ station a esquadra [a delegacia] da polícia

pond a lagoa

pool a piscina

pop music a música pop

popcorn as pipocas

popular popular

port (harbor) o porto

Portugal Portugal

Portuguese português

post [BE] o correio; ~ office os correios

postbox [BE] a caixa do correio

postcard o postal, [o cartão postal]

poster o cartaz

pottery a cerâmica

pound (British sterling) a libra (esterlina)

pregnant a grávida

prescribe prescrever

prescription a receita

press *v* (clothing) passar a ferro [engomar]

pretty bonito

print *v* imprimir [impressar]

prison a prisão

problem o problema

prohibit proibido

pronounce *v* pronunciar

public o público

pull *v* puxar

pump a bomba; ~ (gas) a bomba de gasolina

puncture [BE] o furo

Q

quality a qualidade

quarantine a quarentena

question a pergunta

queue [BE] *n* a fila

quiet sossegado

R

race (cars/horses) a corrida; ~ track o hipódromo

racket (sports) a raquete

railway station [BE] a estação de caminhos de ferro [a estação ferroviária]

rain *v* chover

raincoat a gabardine

rape a violação [o estupro]

rare (unusual) raro [rara]; (steak) mal-passado [mal-passada]

razor a navalha; ~ blade a lâmina de barbear

read *v* ler

ready pronto

real (genuine) de lei

receipt a factura [o recibo]

reception (desk) a recepção

receptionist o/a recepcionista

recommend *v* recomendar

red vermelho

refrigerator o frigorífico [a geladeira]

region a região

regular (gas/petrol) normal

rent *v* alugar

rental car o carro alugado

repair *v* arranjar

repeat *v* repetir

reservation a marcação

reserve *v* reservar

restaurant o restaurante

restroom a casa de banho [o banheiro]

return *v* (come back) voltar; ~ (give back) devolver

right (correct) certo; ~ of way prioridade

ring o anel

river o rio

road a estrada

robbed roubado

robbery o roubo

romantic romântico

room o quarto; **~ service** o serviço
de quarto
round redondo
round-trip de ida e volta
route o caminho
rowboat o barco a remos
rubbish [BE] o lixo; **~ bin [BE]**
o caixote do lixo
ruins as ruínas

S

sad trsite
safe *n* o cofre; *adj* seguro
safety a segurança
sales tax IVA
same o mesmo
sand a areia
sandals as sandálias
sanitary napkin o penso higiénico
[a toalha higiénica]
saucepan o tacho [a caçarola]
sauna o sauna
save guardar
savings account a conta de
poupança
scanner o scanner
scarf o lenço de pescoço
schedule o horário
school a escola
scissors a tesoura
sea o mar
seat o lugar
see *v* ver
self-service self-service
[auto-serviço]
sell *v* vender

send *v* mandar
senior citizen o reformado [oidoso]
separated separado
serious grave/sério
service charge a taxa de serviço
set menu a ementa turística
sex o sexo
sexually transmitted disease (STD)
Doença Sexualmente Transmissível
(DST)
shallow pouco fundo
shampoo o shampoo [o xampu]
sharp afiado [afiada]
shaving cream o creme da barba
sheet o lençol
ship o navio
shirt a camisa
shoe o sapato; **~ store** a sapataria
shopping compras
shopping area a zona comercial
shopping centre [BE] o centro
comercial
shopping mall o centro comercial
short curto
shorts os calções
short sighted [BE] de vistas curtas
show o espectáculo
show mostrar
shower o chuveiro
sick doente
side (of road) o lado
side effect o efeito secundário
side order à parte
side street transversal
sidewalk o passeio
sightseeing tour o circuito turístico

sign o sinal
silk a seda
silver a prata
single (not married) solteiro; ~ room o quarto individual
sink o lava-louças [a pia]
sister a irmã
sit v sentar(-se)
size o número/tamanho
skin a pele
skirt a saia
skis os skis [esquis]
sleep dormir
sleeping bag o saco-cama [osaco de dormir]
sleeper car [BE] couchette [vagão-leitos]
slice a fatia
slippers os chinelos [as pantufas]
slope (ski) a rampa
slow lento
slower mais devagar
slowly devagar
small pequeno
small change troco
smoke v fumar
smoking (area) zona de fumadores [fumantes]
snack bar o snack bar [a lanchonete], a cafetaria
sneakers as sapatilhas [os ténis]
snorkel mergulho sem garrafa [snorkel]
snow a neve
snow v nevar
snowboard a prancha de snowboard

soap o sabonete
soccer o futebol
sock a peúga; meia [meia curta]
soft drink (soda) o refresco
sold out a lotação esgotada
someone alguém
something alguma coisa
sometimes às vezes
son o filho
sore throat a dor de garganta
sorry desculpe
south sul
souvenir a lembrança
spa a estância termal; as termas [spa]
speak falar
speed limit o limite de velocidade
speed v ir com excesso de velocidade
spell soletrar
spend gastar
spine a espinha
sponge a esponja
sport o desporto [o esporte]
sporting goods store a loja de artigos de desporto [esportivos]
spring a primavera
square o quadrado
stadium o estádio
stairs as escadas
stamp o selo
start começar
starter [BE] hors-d'oeuvre; o aperitivo
station a estação
station wagon a carrinha [minivan]
statue a estátua
stay permanecer

steal roubar

steep íngreme

sting o espeto

stolen roubado

stomach o estômago

stop n (bus/tram) a paragem [parada]

stop v parar

store guide a planta da loja

storey [BE] o prédio

straight ahead sempre em frente

stream o ribeiro

street a estrada

stroller a cadeira de bebé [neném]

student o/a estudante

study v estudar

subway o metro; ~ station a estação de metro

suit o fato [o terno]

suitcase a mala de viagem

sun o sol

sun block o protector solar

sunbathe tomar banho de sol

sunburn a queimadura de sol

sunglasses os óculos de sol

super (fuel) super

supermarket o supermercado

surfboard a prancha de surf

sweatshirt a sweatshirt [blusa de moleton]

sweet (taste) doce

sweets [BE] os rebuçados [as balas]

swim v nadar

swimsuit o fato [maiô] de banho

symbol o símbolo

synagogue a sinagoga

table a mesa

tablet (medicine) o comprimido

take v (carry) levar; (medicine) tomar; (time) demorar

take away [BE] para levar

tampons os tampões higiénicos

taste v provar

taxi o táxi; ~ stand a praça [o ponto] de táxis

team a equipa [o time]

teaspoon a colher de chá

telephone o telefone

tennis o ténis

tent a tenda; ~ peg a cavilha; ~ pole a estaca

terminal (airport) o terminal

text v (send a message) escrever uma mensagem; ~ n (message) texto

thank you obrigado

that esse, essa

theater teatro

theft roubo

there ali

thief ladrão

thigh coxa

thirsty com sede

this este, esta

throat a garganta

ticket o bilhete; ~ machine a máquina de venda de bilhetes; ~ office a bilheteira [a bilheteria]

tie (clothing) a gravata

time as horas

timetable [BE] o horário

tire o pneu

tired cansado

tissue o lenço de papel

today hoje

toe o dedo do pé

together juntos

toilet a casa de banho

toilet paper o papel higiénico

tomorrow amanhã

tongue a língua

tonight hoje à noite; for ~ para hoje à noite

too (much) demasiado; ~ (also) também

tooth o dente

toothbrush a escova de dentes

toothpaste a pasta de dentes

tour avisita

tourist o/a turista

towel a toalha

town a cidade; ~ hall a câmara municipal; ~ map o mapa de cidade

toy o brinquedo

toy store o armazém [a loja] de brinquedos

track o trilho

traffic o trânsito; ~ jam o engarrafamento; ~ circle a rotunda; ~ light o semáforo

trail o caminho; ~ map o mapa

train o comboio [o trem]; ~ station a estação de caminho de ferro [a estação ferroviária]

transfer (plane/train) o transbordo

translate v traduzir

trash o lixo; ~ can a lixeira

travel agency a agência de viagens

travel v viajar

traveler's check o cheque de viagens

tree a árvore

trip a excursão

trolley o carrinho

trousers [BE] as calças

T-shirt a T-Shirt [a camiseta]

TV a televisão [a TV]

type o tipo

tyre [BE] o pneu

U

ugly feio

United Kingdom (U.K.) o Reino Unido

umbrella (rain) o guarda-chuva

unbranded medication [BE] o medicamento genérico

uncle o tio

unconscious perder os sentidos

underground [BE] o metropolitano; ~ station a estação de motropolitano

underpants as cuecas

understand compreende

United States os Estados Unidos

university a universidade

unleaded (gas) sem chumbo

unlimited (mileage) sem limite (de quilometragem)

unlock v abrir

upper superior

upstairs em cima

use *v* usar

use *n* uso

useful útil

username o nome de utilizador

utensil o utensílio

V

vacancy o quarto vago

vacation as férias

vaccination a vacinação

vacuum cleaner o aspirador

vagina a vagina

valid válido

valley o vale

valuable de valor

value o valor

VAT (sales tax) IVA

vegetarian vegetariano

vehicle o veículo; ~ registration os documentos do carro

veterinarian o veterinário a veterinária

view point [BE] o miradouro

village a aldeia

vineyard a vinha

visa o visto

visit *n* a visita

visit *v* visitar

visitor center o centro de acolhimento

visually impaired os invisuais

vitamin a vitamina

volleyball o voleibol

vomit vomitar

W

wait esperar

waiting room a sala de espera

waiter o empregado [o garcon]

waitress a empregada [a garçonete]

wake-up call a chamada para despertar

walk *v* dar um passeio

walking passear; ~ boots as botas para caminhar

walking route o itinerário a pé

wall a parede

wallet a carteira (de documentos)

warm *adj* morno

warm *v* aquecer

wash *v* lavar

washing machine a máquina de lavar

watch o relógio

watch *v* ver

water a água

water skis os skis aquáticos [os esquis-aquáticos]

weather o tempo; ~ forecast a previsão do tempo

wedding o casamento; ~ ring a aliança

week a semana

weekend o fim-de-semana

weekly (ticket) semanal

welcome benvindo

west oeste

what que

wheelchair a cadeira de rodas; ~ ramp a rampa para cadeira de rodas

when quando
where onde
white branco
who quem
wife a mulher [a esposa]
window a janela; ~ **(store)** a montra
window seat o lugar à janela
windshield o pára-brisas
windsurfer a prancha à vela
wireless sem fios; ~ **internet** internet sem fios; ~ **internet service** serviçode internet sem fios; ~ **phone** telephone sem fios
with com
without sem
woman a mulher
wool a lã
work *v* **(job)** trabalhar; ~ **(function)** funcionar

wrap *v* embrulhar
wrist o pulso
write *v* escrever
wrong errado

Y

year o ano
yellow amarelo
yes sim
young jovem
youth hostel a pousada [o albergue] da juventude

Z

zebra crossing [BE] a passadeira [a faixa de pedestres]
zero zero
zone a zona
zoo o jardim zoológico; o zoo

Portuguese–English Dictionary

A

à tarde p.m.
a abadia abbey
o abajur lampshade
aberto open
o abraço hug
abril April
acampar camp
o acesso para deficientes access for handicapped
achados e perdidos lost and found
o açougue butcher (Braz.)
o acrílico acrylic
o açúcar sugar
adiante ahead
a admissão admissions
o advogado attorney
o aeroporto airport
a agência de câmbio currency exchange office
a agência de viagem travel agent
agora now
agosto August
a água potável drinking water
o albergue de juventude youth hostel
a aldeia village
a alergia allergy
alérgico allergic
a alfândega customs
o algodão cotton

alguém someone
o alojamento accommodations
alpinismo mountaineering
aluga-se for rent
alugam-se carros car rental
aluguer [aluguel] de bicicletas bicycle rental
amanhã tomorrow
a ambulância ambulance
o andebol handball
antiguidades antiques
aquecer warm
a areia sand
o armazém department store
o ascensor elevator
o aspirador vacuum
a assinatura signature
atender answer
o atendimento admissions
o atendimento ao cliente customer service
atrasado delayed
o atrelado trailer
a auto-estrada highway [motorway]
o autocarro bus
automático automatic
o automóvel car
o avião plane
o aviso warning

B

a bagagem baggage [luggage]
o balcão de registo check-in counter
o balcão de informações information desk

a balsa ferry (Braz.)
o banco bank
o banheiro bathroom [toilets] (Braz.)
o banho bath
o barbeiro barber
o barco boat
o barco salva-vidas lifeboat
o basebol baseball
o basquetebol basketball
o beijo kiss
bemvindo welcome
a biblioteca library
a bicicleta bicycle
o bilhete electrónico e-ticket
o bilhete semanal weekly ticket
a bilheteira ticket office
o bilhete ticket
os bolsos pockets
a bomba pump
a bomba de gasolina gas [petrol] station
os bombeiros fire department [brigade]
as botas de ski ski boots
o boxe boxing
o briberom baby bottle

C

o cabeleireiro hairdresser
o cabeleireiro de homens barber
o cabelo hair
a cachoeira waterfall (Braz.)
a cadeira de rodas wheelchair
a caixa cashier
o calçado shoes

acalculadora calculator
o calor heat
as calorias calories
a câmara municipal town hall
o câmbio currency exchange office
o camião truck
o caminho path
a camioneta bus [coach]
o camping campsite
o campo de desportos playing field
a cana de pesca fishing rod
o canal canal
cancelado canceled
o candeeiro lamp
o capacete helmet
a capela chapel
o cardápio menu (Braz.)
o carnaval carnival
a carne meat
o carro car
a carta regist[r]ada registered letter
o cartão business card
a carteira wallet
a casa house
a casa de banho bathroom
a casa de câmbio currency exchange office
o casaco coat
o castelo castle
a catedral cathedral
o cavalo horse
a caverna cave
o cemitério cemetery
o cêntimo cent

o centro comercial shopping mall [shopping centre]

o centro da cidade downtown area

o centro desportivo sports center

o centro do povo town square

acerveja beer

o chá tea

o chalé cottage

a chamada gratuita toll-free call

a charcutaria delicatessen

a chave key

as chegadas arrivals (airport)

a chupeta pacifier

o churrasco barbecue

a chuva rain

o chuveiro shower

a cidade city

a cidade antiga old town

o cigarro cigarette

o cinema movie theater [cinema]

a cirurgia surgery

a clínica de saúde health clinic

o cobre copper

o código de área area code

o colete de salvação life jacket

a colina hill

com with

com chumbo leaded

o comboio rápido express train

o comboio suburbano local train

o combustível fuel

completo full

o comprimido pill

o computador computer

a comunhão communion

o condicionador conditioner

a confeitaria pastry shop

congelado frozen

os consertos repairs

constipado constipated

a conta corrente checking [current] account

a conta de poupança savings account

o conteúdo contents

o controle de passaportes passport control

o(s) correio(s) post office

o correio azul express mail

o correio normal regular mail

a corrente lock

os cosméticos cosmetics

a costa coast

o couro leather

o credifone phone card

a criança child

o cuidado caution

os cuidados intensivos intensive care

D

a dança dance

a data date

a data de nascimento date of birth

o deck de automóveis parking deck (Braz.)

de ida e volta round-trip [return]

o dentista dentist

a depilação a cera waxing

o depósito refund

o depósito de bagagem baggage check

descartável disposable
o desconto discount
desembarque arrivals (airport)
o desentupidor plunger
o deserto desert
despachar check (baggage)
o desporto sports
o destino destination
o desvio detour [diversion]
o detergente detergent
devagar slow
a devolução refund
Dezembro December
os dias úteis weekdays
os dicionários dictionaries
a dieta diet
o dietético health food
digital digital
o dique dam
a direcção address
dirija com cuidado drive carefully
dissolver dissolve
a distância distance
os doces candy [sweets]
os documentos de regist[r]o
   registration papers
doméstico domestic
o domingo Sunday
a dor pain
a drogaria drugstore
a duna dune

E

o elevador elevator
em construção under construction

em serviço occupied
a embaixada embassy
a embalagem perdida non-returnable
o embarque departures (airport)
a ementa menu
a ementa turística tourist menu
a emergência emergency
empurrar push
encerrado closed
a encosta perigosa dangerous slope
o endereço address
engraçado cute
a enseada bay
a entrada entrance
a entrada proibida no entry
entrar enter
a entrega de bagagem baggage
   claim
as entregas deliveries
o equipamento de mergulho diving
   equipment
os equipamentos eletrónicos
   electronic goods
o ervanário health food store
a escada rolante escalator
as escadas stairs
escalar climbing
a escarpa cliff
a escola school
o escritório de achados e perdidos
   lost-and-found office
a especialidade da casa house
   specialty
a especialidade da região local
   specialty
o espectáculo show

o espectador spectator
a esquadra da polícia police station
o esqui aquático waterskiing (Braz.)
a esquiagem skiing (Braz.)
os esquis skis (Braz.)
os esquis aquáticos water skis (Braz.)
esta noite this evening
a estação station
a estação de caminhos de ferro train station
a estação de metro subway station
a estação de serviço gas [petrol] station
a estação de ferroviária train station (Braz.)
a estação rodoviária bus [coach] station
o estacionamento parking lot [car park]
o estacionamento para clientes customer parking
estacione aqui park here
o estádio stadium
a estância de saúde health spa
a estância turística tourist resort
o estanho can
a estátua statue
a estrada road
a estrada em construção road under construction
a estrada fechada road closed
o estrangeiro foreign
a estreia premiere
o estreitamento de rua narrow road
o estuário estuary

exclusivo para residentes residents only
exclusivo para pedestres pedestrians only
exclusivo para pessoal autorizado authorized vehicles only
a excursão tour
exige-se a identificação proof of identity required
a exposição exhibition
o extintor (de incêndios) fire extinguisher

F

a fábrica factory
a fábrica manual made by hand
fala-se inglês English spoken
a farmácia drugstore
o farol lighthouse
a fazenda farm (Braz.)
a febre fever
fechado closed
a feira fair
a feira popular amusement park
feito à mão handmade
o feriado nacional national holiday
o ferroviário railroad (Braz.)
Fevereiro February
o fim end
o fim de auto-estrada end of highway [motorway]
a floresta forest
o/a florista florist
o fogo de artifício fireworks
a fonte fountain

a forma form
a fortaleza fortress
o forte fort
a fotocópia photocopy
a fotografia photography
a fralda diaper [nappy]
a frente front
fresco fresh
a fronteira border crossing
a fruta fruit
fumar v smoke
os fumadores smoking (area)
os fumantes smoking (area) (Braz.)
o futebol soccer [football]
o futebol americano American football

G

a galeria de arte art gallery
a garagem garage
a garantia guarantee
a gare platforms
a gasolina gas [petrol]
genuino genuine
o/a gerente manager
a gilete razor (Braz.)
o ginásio gym
o glúten gluten
o golfe golf
a gota drop
grande large
grátis free
gratuito free
a gravata tie
a grávida pregnant

a grelha de churrasco barbecue
o grelhado grilled
a gruta cave
guardar save
o guia de viagem travel guide

H

o helicóptero helicopter
o hipismo horseback riding
o hipódromo racetrack [racecourse]
hoje today
o hóquei hockey
o hóquei no gelo ice hockey
o horário schedule [timetable]
o horário comercial business hours
o horário de abertura opening hours
o horário de visitas visiting hours
o hospital hospital
o hotel hotel

I

ida e volta round-trip [return]
a igreja church
a ilha island
o IVA imposto de venda sales tax [VAT]
incluído included
incluído no preço included in the price
o indicativo code
o infantário kindergarten
as informações information
as informações turísticas tourist information
o ingrediente ingredient

o início de auto-estrada highway [motorway] entrance
inocente innocent
inquebrável unbreakable
inserir v insert
insosso bland
as instruções instructions
integral whole wheat
interdito ao trânsito traffic-free zone
interessado interested
internacional international
introduzir introduce
o inverno winter
o IVA sales tax [VAT]

J

Janeiro January
a janela window
o jardim garden
o jardim botânico botanical garden
o jardim zoológico zoo
a joalharia jeweler
o jogo match
Julho July
Junho June

L

a lã wool
o lago lake
a lancha motorboat
os lanches snacks
o largo square
os lacticínios dairy products
a lavagem de carros car wash
a lavagem de roupa laundry facilities

a lavandaria laundromat [launderette]
la avandaria a seco dry-cleaner
lavar a seco dry-clean only
lavável à máquina machine washable
a lembrança souvenir
a lente lens
as lições lessons
a lima nail file
o limite da cidade city limits
o limite de bagagem baggage allowance
a limpeza cleaning
a língua language
a língua estrangeira foreign language
a linha platform
a linha aérea airline
a linha de bonde tram (Braz.)
a linha férrea railroad [railway]
a liquidação clearance sale
o líquido liquid
Lisboa Lisbon
a lista menu
a lista telefónica directory
a lista de preços price list
o litoral coast
a livraria bookstore
livre vacant
o livrete car registration papers
o loção para depois da barba after-shave lotion
a loja de antiguidades antique store
a loja de artigos de desporto sporting goods store
a loja de brinquedos toy store

a loja de departamentos department store

as lojas duty-free duty-free store

a lotação esgotada sold out

a lotaria lottery

a louça china

o lugar à janela window seat

o lugar na asa aisle seat

o luxo luxury

M

a madeira wood

as madeixas highlights

o maestro conductor

magro fat-free

Maio May

mais more

mais devagar slower

mais rápido faster

as malas luggage [baggage]

mandar send

os mandriões loafers

o mapa da cidade city map

o mapa dos arredores area map

a máquina fotográfica camera

o mar sea

Março March

as massas noodles

a mata wood

a maternidade maternity

a matrícula do automóvel license plate [registration] number

o médico doctor

médio medium

o menu menu

o menu turístico tourist menu

a memória memory

o mercado market

as mercadorias goods

as mercadorias isentas duty-free goods

a mercearia grocer

mergulhar diving

o metro subway [underground]

a mina mine

a missa mass

o mobiliário furniture

a moeda coin

o moinho mill

o moinho de vento windmill

molhada wet

o molusco shellfish

a montanha mountain

o montanhismo mountaineering

o monte hill

o monumento monument

o monumento comemorativo (war) memorial

o morro hill

o mosteiro monastery

a moto de montanha mountain bike

a motorizada motorcycle

os móveis furniture

as mudanças manual shift

a mudança de óleo oil change

mudar change

a mulher woman

a muralha wall

a muralha da cidade city wall

o muro wall

o museu museum
a música music
a música ao vivo live music
a música clássica classical music
a música folk folk music
a música pop pop music

N

nacional national
nacionalidade nationality
nada a declarar nothing to declare
não entre keep out
não fumadores non-smokers
não fumantes non-smokers (Braz.)
não fumar no smoking
não funciona out of order
o Natal Christmas
navegação à vela sailing
o navio ship
a neve snow
o nome name
a nome de família last name
o nome de solteira maiden name
Novembro November
novo new
as nozes nuts
o número de telefone telephone number
o número do passaporte passport number

O

as obras construction
o oculista optician
ocupado occupied

a oferta especial special offer
a oficina office
o óleo oil
o ônibus bus (Braz.)
o ônibus elétrico tram (Braz.)
o operador operator
a ordem de pagamento money order
a orquestra orchestra
a ourivesaria goldsmith
o ouro gold
o outono fall [autumn]
Outubro October

P

o paço palace
a padaria bakery
o país country
o palácio palace
o palácio da justiça law court
o palco stage
o pão bread
o papel higiénico toilet paper
o papel reciclado recycled paper
a papelaria stationery store
para microondas microwaveable
para uso externo external use only
a paragem de autocarro bus stop
o parapente gliding
o pára-quedas parachuting
pare stop
a parede wall
o parque park
o parque de campismo campsite
o parque de diversões amusement park

o parque de estacionamento parking lot [car park]

o parque nacional national park

o parque para clientes customer parking

o parque privativo private parking

as partidas departures (airport)

as partidas internacionais international departures

a Páscoa Easter

a passadeira crosswalk [zebra crossing]

o passageiro passenger

as passagens (airplane) tickets

o passaporte passport

o passe mensal monthly ticket

o passeio walkway

o passeio panorâmico scenic route

o passeio a cavalo horseback riding

o passeio com guia guided tour

o passeio circular round trip

a pastelaria pastry shop

a pastilha lozenge

a patinagem no gelo ice skating

os patins skates

o património do estado public (building)

pedestre pedestrian (Braz.)

o pediatra pediatrician

a pedicure pedicure

o peito chest

a peixaria fish store [fishmonger]

a pensão bed & breakfast

os peões pedestrian

pequeno small

o pequeno-almoço breakfast

o percurso da natureza nature trail

o percurso de bicicleta bike trail

o percurso panorâmico scenic route

perdido lost

o perigo danger

perigoso dangerous

permanecer v stay

a pérola pearl

perto near

a pesca fishing

o pico peak

a pílula pill

o PIN PIN

pintado de fresco wet paint

a piscina swimming pool

a pista de corrida racetrack (Braz.)

a pista de ônibus bus lane (Braz.)

a pista escorregadia slippery road (Braz.)

a pista fechada road closed (Braz.)

a pista simples two-way traffic (Braz.)

o planador gliding

o planetário planetarium

o pneu tire [tyre]

o poço well

pode cozinhar cooking facilities

a polícia police

a polícia de trânsito traffic police

a poltrona seat

a pomada ointment

o pomar orchard

a ponte bridge

a ponte baixa low bridge

a **ponte estreita** narrow bridge
a **ponte levadiça** drawbridge
o **ponto de ônibus** bus stop (Braz.)
o **ponto de táxi** taxi stand [rank] (Braz.)
por favor please
a **porta** door
o **porta-moedas** purse
a **porta de embarque** boarding gate
a **porta de incêndio** fire door
a **portagem** toll
o **portão** gate
a **porta automática** automatic door
o **porto** port
o **posto de ambulância** ambulance
  station
o **posto de gasolna** gas [petrol]
  station (Braz.)
a **pousada** guest house
o **povoado** village
a **praça** square
a **praça de táxis** taxi stand
a **praia** beach
a **praia de nudismo** nudist beach
a **prancha de surf[e]** surfboard
a **prata** silver
o **prato do dia** dish of the day
o **preço** price
preferencial yield [give way]
prejudicado impaired
a **primavera** spring
a **primeira classe** first class
Primeiro do Ano New Year's Day
  (Braz.)
o **primeiro nome** first name
os **primeiros socorros** first aid

a **prioridade** priority
privado private
os **produtos de limpeza** cleaning
  products
o **produto dietético** health food
proibida a entrada no entry
proibido forbidden
proibido acampar no camping
proibido estacionar no parking
proibido fumar no smoking
o **pronto socorro-emergência**
  accident and emergency
o **propósito** purpose
provar v taste
o **próximo** next
puxar pull

Q

a **quantia** fare
quarta-feira Wednesday
o **quartel de bombeiros** fire station
o **quarto duplo** double room
o **quarto para alugar** room to rent
quatro estrelas four star
a **queda de água** waterfall
a **queda de pedras** falling rocks
o **quilómetro** kilometer
a **quinta** farm
quinta-feira Thursday
o **quiosque de jornais** newsagent

R

os **raios-x** x-ray
a **rampa** ramp

a receita federal customs control
a recepção reception
o recibo receipt
reciclado recycled
reduza a velocidade slow down
o reembolso refund
as refeições meals
o regente conductor (music)
a região region
o relicário shrine
as reparações repairs (car)
a represa dam
o rés-do-chão first floor
reservado reserved
a reserva reservation
o reservatório reservoir
residencial guest house
o restaurante restaurant
retire fundos withdraw money
retire o bilhete take ticket
retornar v return
a revista magazine
a ribeira stream
o rio river
o rochedo cliff
o rolo film (camera)
a rota alternada alternate route
a rotunda traffic circle [roundabout]
a roupa interior underwear
a rua street
a rua fechada ao trânsito road closed
a rua principal main road
a rua com sentido único one-way street
as ruínas ruins

S

sábado Saturday
o sabonete soap
o saco bag
a saída exit
a saída de emergência emergency exit
o sal salt
a sala de operações operating room
s sala de concertos concert hall
s sala de espera waiting room
o saldo sale
a salsicharia delicatessen
o salva-vidas lifeguards
o sapato shoe
a sé cathedral
o secador de cabelo hair dryer
a seda silk
a segunda classe second class
o segundo andar second floor
segunda-feira Monday
os segundos seconds
a segurança security
o seguro insurance
o selo stamp
sem açúcar sugar-free
sem álcool alcohol-free
sem cafeína caffeine-free
sem chumbo unleaded
sem gordura fat-free
sem sal salt-free
o semáforo traffic light
a semana week

a senha ticket
as senhoras ladies
a serra mountain range
o serviço service charge
o serviço a clientes customer service
o serviço de quarto room service
o serviço incluído service included
Setembro September
sexta-feira Friday
o silêncio silence
a sinaleira traffic light (Braz.)
só a dinheiro cash only
a sobremesa dessert
a soirée evening performance
o solário sun lounge
o solo escorregadio slippery road surface
o solteiro single (room)
o sombreiro umbrella (Braz.)
o sopa soup
sos emergency services (Port.)
o suco fruit juice (Braz.)
o supermercado supermarket

T

os talheres utensils [cutlery]
o talho butcher
a tarifa rate
a tarifa de pedágio toll (Braz.)
a tarifa mínima minimum charge
a taxa de serviço service charge
o táxi taxi
o taxímetro taxi meter
o teatro theater
o teatro ao ar livre a open-air theater

o teatro infantil children´s theater
o teleférico chair lift
o telefone telephone
o telefone de emergência emergency telephone
o telefone público public telephone
o telefone residencial home phone number
o telefonista operator
os temperos spices
o templo temple
a tenda tent
o ténis tennis
a terapia intensiva intensive care
terça-feira Tuesday
as termas spa
o terminal terminal
a tipografia printing
as toalhas linen
o toldo awning
tóxico toxic
o tráfego lento slow traffic
o trailer trailer
o trajecto do autocarro bus route
o trampolim diving board
transferir transfer
o trânsito impedido closed to traffic
transportar carry
o tratamento treatment
o travão brake
o travão de emergência emergency brake
o trem expresso express train (Braz.)
o trem local local train (Braz.)
to revo intersection [crossroad] (Braz.)
o trigo wheat

o trolley-carro tram
o túmulo grave
o túnel tunnel
o turismo tourist information office

U

a universidade university
os utensílios de cozinha kitchen equipment
os utensílios domésticos household goods

V

o vagão-cama sleeping car
o vagão restaurante dining car
a vaga vacancy (Braz.)
vago vacant
o vale valley
o vale postal money order
válido valid
a varanda balcony
os vegetais vegetables
o veículo vehicle
o veículo lento slow vehicle
o veleiro sailboat
a velocidade máxima maximum speed limit
a venda de bilhetes ticket office

venenoso poisonous
o verão summer
o verdadeiro real
o verdureiro fruit and vegetable store (Braz.)
o vestuário fitting room
a via de dois sentidos two-way traffic
a via de sentido único one-way street
a via rápida highway [motorway]
a via turística scenic route
o vidro glass
o vidro reciclado recycled glass
a vila town
o vilarejo village
as vinhas vineyard
o vinho do porto port (wine)
o vinho wine
a visita guiada guided tour
o voleibol volleyball
o vôo flight

Z

a zona aduaneira customs zone
a zona comercial business district
a zona de pedestres pedestrian zone
a zona histórica historic area
a zona residencial residential zone